The Greenwich Pensioners V1

Lieutenant Hatchway

In the interest of creating a more extensive selection of rare historical book reprints, we have chosen to reproduce this title even though it may possibly have occasional imperfections such as missing and blurred pages, missing text, poor pictures, markings, dark backgrounds and other reproduction issues beyond our control. Because this work is culturally important, we have made it available as a part of our commitment to protecting, preserving and promoting the world's literature. Thank you for your understanding.

THE

GREENWICH PENSIONERS.

BY

LIEUT. HATCHWAY, R.N.

> We 'll gar the callants a' look blue,
> An' sing anither tune:
> They 're blessing aye o' what they 'll do;
> We 'll tell them what we 've dune!
> DOUBLEDAY.

IN THREE VOLUMES.
VOL. I.

LONDON:
HENRY COLBURN, PUBLISHER,
13, GREAT MARLBOROUGH STREET.
1838.

LONDON:
PRINTED BY STEWART AND MURRAY,
OLD BAILEY.

PREFACE.

The reasons which induce the author of the following sketches to appear before the public are various; yet they proceed from no overweening conceit of his own powers, nor from any wish to pluck a leaf from the laurels of the talented naval writers who have preceded him; but having had opportunities of acquiring a knowledge of his particular subject, arising from a long and familiar intercourse with "Greenwich Pensioners," he trusts he has, on that plea, some claim to the attention of an indulgent public.

In a few short years, the race who in the late long, and eventful war, fought our country's battles, and shed their best blood in its defence, will have disappeared entirely from the earth; it, therefore, behoves us to preserve, even though in the garb of fiction, their narratives and histories. This is the author's design, and although in the present series he may have given much attention to effect, yet it has been his greatest wish to confirm that which is true, and deny that which is incorrect. He cannot be made answerable for the veracity of all his story-tellers, nor does he demand for them a very exorbitant degree of reliance: it is well known that eye-witnesses will each, in some small degree, be found to vary, in their relations of what they have witnessed, and we cannot, therefore, be surprised if, after the lapse of many years, we should meet with many omissions of facts, and some overcharged representations. The author does not aim at the precision of an historian—being studious rather to please, while he only suggests facts, which are better known, and more authentically related, by those to whose province they belong. He has been duly cautious not to rely implicitly on his heroes, when they have been found greatly at variance with generally received opinions; but, in order that a fair judgment should be attainable, he has occasionally introduced, and placed in juxta-position, the jarring versions.

The commencement of these volumes appeared in four numbers of the United Service Journal, under the title of "Stories of Greenwich;" but, being desirous of presenting a more complete picture than could well be done in short, occasional papers, the author came to the determination of endeavouring to produce the work which he now submits; and he confidently hopes that a portion of the kind patronage which is in general so liberally bestowed, will be awarded to the " Greenwich Pensioners."

GREENWICH, 1838.

ACCOUNT

OF

GREENWICH HOSPITAL,

FROM ITS FOUNDATION TO THE PRESENT TIME.[*]

THE first idea of founding an Hospital, for the reception of seamen, worn out, or wounded and disabled in their country's service, is ascribed, with every appearance of justice, to the pious, and humane Queen Mary, consort of William III. The extreme difficulty, and numerous impediments, in the way of found-

---

[*] Principally compiled from the Works of N. Hawksmoor, Esq., Clerk of the Works of the Hospital, published in 1728, and of the Rev. Messrs. Cook and Maule, Chaplains of the Hospital, published in 1789.

ing so extensive an Hospital as that proposed, arising out of the poverty of the realm, and its unsettled state, must be evident to every one conversant with the political history of the period; and the benevolence and firmness of purpose evinced by the Queen, under the trying circumstances by means of which they were at length surmounted, demand the warmest praise and admiration. It is to her piety and wisdom, that the Hospital owes its foundation; but England's pride and glory united in maturing the design, and in rendering the noble pile what it now is—an object of wonder and envy to foreigners, and of veneration and pleasure to Englishmen.

The site of Greenwich Hospital was previously occupied by the ancient palace of Placentia, the building of which was commenced in the reign of Henry VI., by Humphrey Duke of Gloucester, and finished, after a lapse of more than sixty years, by Henry VII. It is said to have received its name "Placentia," from the pleasantness of its situation, and the beautiful gardens and park attached to it.

The palace, together with the manors of Lewisham and East Greenwich, being conveyed over to Henry VIII., his heirs and successors, in the 22nd year of his reign; that prince spared no cost to enlarge and adorn it, and to make it "a splendid and magnificent palace." He used it also as his favourite residence.

In this palace were born Henry VIII., and his brother Edmund; Edward VI., Queen Mary, Elizabeth of glorious memory, and several children of King James I. Here also died, the youthful and promising sovereign, Edward VI.

The palace, from a drawing of it now extant, possessed few architectural beauties; having been apparently built without any real design, and enlarged to suit the occasion. At the east end were several small buildings erected by Henry VII., for the use of a community of friars, who probably were astronomers.

During the embarrassments of the Commonwealth, the Parliament came to the resolution in 1652, that, "Greenwich House, Park, and lands, should be immediately sold for ready money;" and surveyors were appointed for the due valuation of the premises: which survey, and sale, were afterwards ordered to be carried into execution. Times like those were, however, unfavourable to the design, and no one was found willing to make the purchase; so that at the restoration of Charles II., the property, though in a very dilapidated and neglected condition, continued to be the property of the crown.

King Charles, finding the palace in such a state as to be wholly uninhabitable, determined on its demolition, and on erecting a more suitable residence on its site. In the Diary of Pepys, is the following note;— "4th March, 1663-4. At Greenwich, I observed the foundation laying of a very great house for the king, which will cost a great deal of money;" and again, "July 26th, 1665. To Greenwich,— the king mightily pleased with his new buildings there."

King Charles, however, did not live to complete his palace, but left it in an unfinished state at his death, probably from the want of funds; and it remained in that condition until after the glorious revolution, and the accession to the throne of England of William and Mary. The Palace was designed by the celebrated Inigo Jones, and erected by Mr. Webb.

It appears by the original "grant," that, on the 25th October, in the sixth year of the reign of William and Mary, 1694, the unfinished palace, with large additions of lands on the eastward, and as far as the still existing "Fryers Road," on the westward, were, by letters patent under the great seal, made over to trustees for the formation of an Hospital, having for its object, "The relief, and support of seamen, serving on board the shipps and vessells belonging to the Navy Royall, who by reason of age, woundes, or other disabilities" were "uncapable of further service at sea:" and that, on the 12th day of March following, King William issued his royal "Commission."—his "most deare consort" being dead—to his "dearly beloved brother-in-law Prince George, hereditary of Denmark," in conjunction with many others, including the most noble in the land; constituting and appointing them, Commissioners, for putting "the said good and pious purposes in execucion."

In this commission His Majesty rehearses the claims of the old and worn out sailor, in the following memorable words:—"And Whereas, the seafaring men of this Kingdome have for a long time distinguisht themselves throughout the world, by their industry and skillfullnesse in their proper employments, and by their courage and constancy manifested in engagementes and hazardes for the defence (and) honour of their native country: And, nothing is more likely to continue this their ancient reputacion, and to invite greater numbers of our subjects to betake themselves to the sea, then the makeing some competent provision, that seamen, who by age, woundes, or other accidentes shall become disabled for further service at sea, and shall not be in a condicion to maintaine themselves comfortably, may not fall under hardships and miseries, but may be supported at the Publick Charge: And, that the children of such disabled seamen, And also, the widowes and children of such seamen as shall happen to be slaine in sea service, may in some reasonable manner be provided for and educated: Wee have determined to erect and establish a Hospitall," &c. &c.

In pursuance of the above Commission, a number of those constituted by it Commissioners and Trustees, met at Guildhall on the 17th May, 1695, and appointed a Committee to view the premises included in the grant of William and Mary for the purpose: which Committee reported, that, by the addition of a wing, it would be capable of accommodating between three and four hundred men.

The barbarous intention was, it is said, seriously entertained by one party, of demolishing the Palace entirely, and erecting a building on a far inferior scale. The project went so far, that it was proposed to Her Majesty Queen Mary, a short time previous to her decease, and happily frustrated by the firmness of her reply; for no arguments for taking it down could prevail. "Her Majesty," says Mr. Hawksmoor, "received the project of pulling down that wing, with as much indignation, as her excellent temper would suffer her, ordered it should remain, and the other side of the Royal Court made answerable to it in proper time."

The immediate conduct of the building was entrusted to a committee of sixty, who fixed upon Mr. John Scarborough to be clerk of the works; Sir Christopher Wren, the King's Surveyor-General, having generously undertaken, gratuitously, the office of architect, or surveyor. The foundations of the new base building were accordingly laid in due form by the committee on the 3d June, 1696, and completed in 1698.

The Painted Hall, intended to be the refectory of the officers and pensioners, was then commenced, and prosecuted with so much industry, that the dome was erected, and the whole roofed in, by August, 1703.

At about the same time the foundations of the N. E., or Queen Anne's, Building, corresponding to King Charles's, were also laid.

In 1699 great part of the foundations of the Eastern Colonnade and of the Chapel were laid; but funds were wanting to carry on the works, and they proceeded so slowly, that it was not until 1725 that the raising the west front of Queen Anne's Quarter, whose foundations had been laid twenty-seven years previously, was commenced, and the building was not completed till 1728.

In 1752, Queen Mary's, or the S. E. quarter, containing the Chapel, was finished; the rents and profits of the Derwentwater estates, forfeited by the treason of the Earl, having, in 1735, been made over to the directors by the Parliament for that purpose, as well as 6,000*l.* per annum from the coal and culm tax.

The general plan of the buildings appears to have had reference to the house still standing, now used as the school for girls in the Royal Naval Asylum, called the Queen's House, which was a favourite residence of her Majesty Queen Mary. Her fondness for this villa induced her, it is said, to wish to preserve a passage to it through the Hospital from the river; and thus, out of what is handed down to us as an act of royal caprice, such " a combination and a form" of beauty and grandeur have been attained, as are rarely to be met with.

Having thus given a concise account of the Hospital from its foundation, it is hoped a statement of its present condition will not be uninteresting.

The visitor entering the Hospital from the river, or North Gate, is received on a broad gravelled terrace, running parallel to the river, 865 feet in length, having at each end a pavilion, built in 1778, and dedicated to their Majesties George III. and Queen Charlotte.

On the right hand is the original building, King Charles's Palace; on the left, Queen Anne's Building, distant from each other 273 feet. Between these buildings are neat and well trimmed grass-plots, surrounded by chains, suspended by granite pillars chiseled in imitation of cannon.

The square is intersected by broad foot-paths, and in its centre is a statue of King George II., executed by Rysbrach, and carved out of a block of marble said to have been taken from the French by Admiral Sir George Rooke, and to have weighed eleven tons. The statue was presented to the Hospital by Admiral Sir John Jennings, at that time the "Master and Governor," in token of the respect he entertained for his Royal master. It represents his Majesty in the habit of a Roman emperor, and is a great ornament to the square. On each side the base of the statue are inscribed the following Latin mottoes:—[*]

---

[*] The Latin inscriptions were selected by Mr. Stanyan, author of "Grecian Antiquities": the Translations are by a talented member of the Cambridge University.

ON THE EAST SIDE.

Hic requies senectæ
His modus lasso maris et viarum
Militiæq.

which may be thus translated :—

Rest to the aged here: the end of toil
To mariners, whom journeyings in the deep
And war's alarms have wearied.

ON THE WEST SIDE.

Fessos tuto placidissima portu
Accipit.

Quiet retreat! that gives the weary rest,
Within its grateful haven.

ON THE NORTH SIDE.

Hic ames dici pater atq. princeps.

Father! and Prince! may'st thou well pleased receive,
The merited address.

And underneath the Royal Standard :—

Imperium pelagi.
The Empire of the Sea!

ON THE SOUTH SIDE.

Principi potentissimo
Georgio IIdo.
Britanniarum regi,
Cujus auspiciis et patrocinio
Augustissimum hoc hospitium
Ad sublevandos militantium
in classe emeritorium

Labores —— a regiis ipsius antecessoribus
fundatum
Auctius indius et splendidies
exurgit,
JOHANNES JENNINGS, Eques.
Ejusdem hospitii præfectus,
Iconem hanc pro debitâ suâ
Erga principem reverentiâ
Et patriam charitate
posuit,
Anno Domini
MDCCXXXV.

To the most powerful Prince
GEORGE II.
King of Great Britain:
Under whose auspices and patronage,
This most magnificent Hospital,
For relieving the distresses
Of well-deserving Sailors—
Founded
By His royal predecessors—
Is daily becoming more vast,
And noble,
Sir JOHN JENNINGS, Knight,
Governor of the Hospital,
In token of respect due to his Prince,
And of affection to his Country,
Erected this Statue.
A. D. 1735.

Passing down the centre of the Grand Square, you approach the Painted Hall on the right, and the

Chapel on the left hand, surmounted with their beautiful domes, and on either hand, in continuation, are handsome colonnades, composed of upwards of three hundred duplicated stone pillars and pilasters twenty feet high; the ascent being by a double flight of stone steps, occupying the whole extent of the opening.

Beyond the Hospital is the centre building of the Naval Asylum, or the Queen's House, which, although built by Inigo Jones, bears very slight, if any, marks of his genius. Above, the sight is bounded by the Royal Observatory in the Park.

The Hospital alone covers an extent of nearly twenty acres, and is separated from the schools, infirmary, &c., by walls and iron railings. Plans are, however, on foot for enclosing the Infirmary; and this will, when carried into effect, be a very great improvement, by shewing to better advantage the architectural beauties of the Hospital.

The principal entrances are the North, South, East, and West Gates. The West Gate is the grand entrance, and is formed by two rusticated stone pillars, with iron gates, having the porter's lodge and a small guard-room adjoining.

The piers are embellished with sculpture of implements of war, and are surmounted by two large stone globes, terrestrial and celestial, six feet in diameter. The globes are placed in an oblique position, agreeably to the latitude of their situation, and are correctly delineated with the meridional and tropical circles, &c. On the terrestrial globe the outlines of land and sea were originally traced, together with the track of Lord Anson round the world in H.M.S. Centurion, but time has almost completely obliterated them.

At the East Gate the piers are open iron work.

King Charles's, or the N.W. quarter, is substantially built of Portland stone, and rusticated. It is in a high state of preservation, and only lately required new roofing. In the middle, on the eastern front, facing the Grand Square, is a tetrastyle portico of the Corinthian order, crowned with its proper entablature and a pediment. At each end is a pavilion, formed by four corresponding pilasters of the same order, with a balustrade. In the tympanum of the pediment is a piece of sculpture, consisting of two figures, the one representing "*Fortitude,*" the other "*Dominion of the Sea.*"

The north or river front presents the appearance of two similar pavilions, each having its proper pediment, supported by a range of the same Corinthian columns before mentioned, and their entablature. Over the portal joining these pavilions are ornaments of festoons and flowers.

In the tympanum of the eastern pediment, (part of the Palace,) is a piece of sculpture representing *Mars* and *Fame*, and in the frieze the following inscription:—

CAROLUS II. REX.

A. REG. XVI.

which agrees with Mr. Pepys' note as to the date of the building. The south front corresponds with the north.

The western side was originally of brick, which, going rapidly to decay, was in 1810 taken down and re-erected on an enlarged and more suitable scale. It is now of Portland stone, in the Corinthian order. The centre is supported by six columns, over which is an attic, containing a large pannel for the receipt of sculpture. The remainder of the façade is decorated with pilasters of the same order, crowned with balustrades. In the frieze is the following:—

GEORGIUS III. REX.

A. REGNI 55, A.D. MDCCCXIV.

The N.E. angle of this building is appropriated as the Governor's House, and part of the N.Western as the Lieutenant-Governor's. In this is also a ward called King Charles's Ward, occupying, with the exception of the Governor's House, the whole extent of the building. It is open to the inspection of visitors, and contains many interesting curiosities.

Queen Anne's Quarter corresponds, with a few slight variations, to King Charles's, and furnishes apartments for eleven officers, civil and military, and lodges 434 men.*

---

* In this quarter is the Anson Ward, wherein is deposited the figure-head of H.M.S. Centurion, the ship in which Lord Anson circumnavigated the globe in 1744. This ponderous relic was preserved and erected in Goodwood Park; it was afterwards transferred to Windsor, from whence it was sent to Greenwich by order of his late Majesty William IV. The following lines are the production of an *old* poet and pensioner:—

THE POOR LION,
Snug at Last.

Brave Anson, foundered, left poor I alone,
Death boarded his prize, and claimed him as his own!
How I've been boxed about, pray, reader, mark!
Long stationed at Chichester—next Windsor Park
—Shatter'd and old, a GRACIOUS FRIEND I found,
His royal hand has raised me from the ground;
I've been repaired, and fitted out so clever,
And look as bold, and am as fierce as ever.

Finally,

Our beloved SAILOR KING, has moored me here
Alongside the jolly pensioners in Greenwich tier.

Anson Ward, 1834.   JOSEPH SPENCER.

To the southward of these are King William's and Queen Mary's Buildings. King William's contains the Great, or Painted Hall, with its vestibule and dome, designed and erected by Sir Christopher Wren. The tambour of the dome is formed by a circle of columns, duplicated, of the composite order, with four projecting groups of columns at the quoins. The attic above is a circle without breaks, covered with the dome, and terminated with a turret.

The west front is of brick, and was finished by Sir John Vanburgh, at that time surveyor of the Hospital. In the middle is a magnificent tetrastyle frontispiece, of the Doric order, the columns of which are six feet in diameter, and well proportioned, with an entablature, &c., the whole of Portland stone. At each end of this front is a pavilion, crowned with a circular pediment; and in that at the north end is a piece of sculpture, consisting of groups of marine trophies, and four large heads, embossed, representing the four winds, with a sealion, and unicorn.

In the tympanum of the pediment of the Western Colonnade, facing King William's Square, is presented an emblematical representation of the death of Nelson, in alto relievo.[*] The north and south fronts are of

---

[*] The following explanation of this work of art is extracted from the description of the Hospital, sold at the Painted Hall.

stone; the windows decorated with architraves and imposts rusticated, and the walls crowned with cornices.

The S.E., or Queen Mary's quarter contains the Chapel, with its vestibule and cupola, corresponding with that over the Painted Hall. It was intended that this building should have been like King William's in every respect, but more regard having been paid to convenience than ornament, the whole front is of Portland stone, and in a plain style.

THE CHAPEL.

The entrance to the Chapel is by an octangular

—"In the centre is placed Britannia, resting upon a rock, washed by the ocean, and receiving the dead body of Nelson, delivered to her by one of the attendant Tritons. Victory, with her right hand, supports the body of the hero, and with her left, resigns to Britannia the trident of the god, in token of dominion of the sea. Behind Neptune, who is seated in his hell, drawn by sea horses, is seen a British sailor, announcing 'Trafalgar' as the scene of the hero's death. On the left hand of Britannia is represented a naval genius, recording the victories of the 'Nile' and 'Copenhagen;' before whom is a British Lion, holding in his paws a tablet, inscribed 'Nelson's cxxii Battles:' adjoining these are the sister kingdoms— England, Ireland, and Scotland, with their appropriate emblems, the rose, thistle, and shamrock, reclining affectionately on each other, and overcome by feelings of the deepest sorrow."

vestibule, in which are four niches containing statues of Faith, Hope, Charity, and Meekness, beautifully wrought in artificial stone, from the designs of B. West. The ascent into the chapel is accomplished by a semicircular flight of fourteen granite steps.

Over the portal is the following beautiful and appropriate text :—

"Let them give thanks whom the Lord hath redeemed and delivered from the hand of the enemy."—*Psalm* 107.

The portal consists of an architrave, frieze, and cornice of statuary marble, the jambs of which are in one piece, and twelve feet in height, enriched with excellent sculpture by Bacon. The great folding doors are of solid mahogany, elegantly carved.

Within is a portico formed by six fluted marble columns, whose capitals and bases are Ionic, after Greek models. They support the organ gallery, and are crowned with an entablature and balustrades suitably ornamented.

Under this portico, on the left hand side of the entrance, is a brilliantly executed marble bust of the late Governor, Admiral Sir R. G. Keats, by Chantrey, presented by his late Majesty William IV., and placed there by his royal command, with an accompanying inscription, conveying a mark of esteem and condescension rarely paid by a sovereign to a subject.

On each side the organ gallery are four grand Corinthian columns, twenty-eight feet in height, their shafts of scagliola in imitation of Sienna marble, by Richter, their capitals and bases being of statuary marble; and at the further end of the Chapel are four others to correspond.

Above the galleries is a richly carved stone fascia, on which stands a range of pilasters of the composite order, their shafts being also of scagliola, corresponding with the columns, which together appear to support the epistylium surrounding the Chapel. The epistylium is ornamented with angels, bearing festoons of oak leaves, dolphins, shells, &c., and supports an arched ceiling, enriched in the antique style, with foliage, golochi, &c., and divided into compartments.

The Chapel is adorned with numerous paintings in chiaro'scuro, representing the prophets, the apostles, and evangelists, and illustrative of some of the principal events in the life of our Saviour. They are all from West's designs, and executed in a superior style by De Bruyn, Catton, Milburne, and Rebecca.

The pulpit is of satin-wood, and circular, supported by six fluted columns of lime tree, with an entablature above, richly carved. Between the columns are tablets in alto relievo, from West's designs, having for their subjects the acts of the Apostles. The reading desk is also of satin-wood, and square, having on either side alto relievos of the prophets Daniel, Micah, Zachariah, and Malachi.

The communion table, a semi-oval slab of white marble, is light, elegant, and unostentatious; the ascent is by black marble steps, and the rail around it is formed of graceful festoons of ears of corn and bunches of grapes. Above, in a richly carved and gilt frame, terminated in a semicircle, is a large painting by West, twenty-five feet high, and fourteen in width, representing the preservation of St. Paul from shipwreck on the island of Malta. The painting is generally considered good.

On either side the arch formed by the upper part of the altar-piece are angels of statuary marble by Bacon, also from West's designs; one bearing the cross, and the other the elements of the eucharist. The whole is terminated above, in the segment between the great cornice and the ceiling, by a painting in chiaro'scuro; forming the last of, the series of events in the life of our Saviour, and commemorating his ascension.

The organ is one of the finest toned in England, and has lately undergone a complete repair.

The aisle and the spaces round the altar and organ-gallery are paved with black and white marble, in golochi, frets, and other ornaments, having in the centre a representation of an anchor and mariner's compass, composed of the same materials. The Chapel will contain about twelve hundred of the pensioners and nurses, and is furnished with galleries, wherein are seats for the officers and their families.

The interior and roof of this Chapel were entirely destroyed by a fire, which took place on the 2d January, 1779.* It is, however, well restored, from

---

* The particulars of this destructive fire are given in the following extract from the *Annual Register*:—" 2nd January, 1779. At six o'clock in the morning, a dreadful fire broke out at Greenwich Hospital, which burned most furiously. At ten o'clock, the Chapel, (the most beautiful in the kingdom, the dome on the south-east quarter of the building, and the great dining-hall, were entirely consumed. The reservoirs at the top of the building were unfortunately almost empty, and no water to be had for some time but by a line of pensioners, who handed buckets from the Thames, but the supply was so very inadequate that the fire raged with unrestrained fury for several hours. A great many of the wards were destroyed, and the west wing, in which is the beautiful painted hall, was in great danger, as the wind was blowing that way. About eleven o'clock several engines arrived from London, but the fire was not got under till the evening. The damage done is immense, and it will cost a very large sum to restore that part of the Hospital to its former beauty and elegance.

designs of James Stuart, Esq., at that time the surveyor of the Hospital.

THE PAINTED HALL.

This was originally built for, and at one time used as, a dining hall for the pensioners. It consists of three apartments—the vestibule, the grand hall or saloon, and the upper hall, intended as a refectory for the officers, (after the manner of the Hotel des Invalides at Paris.)

The vestibule measures fifty-two feet by twenty-one, and is lighted by a beautiful lanthorn, surmounted by the dome. In the cupola is painted a compass, with its proper points duly bearing, and in the wings, in chiaro'scuro, the four winds, with their respective attributes.

At the base of the windows, around the interior, are suspended the colours of the Royal Marines, placed there in 1827 by order of His late Majesty when Lord

---

The fire began in the tailors' shop, wherein the men had been at work the preceding day, but had mingled holiday rejoicing too much with their labours. The following wards are burnt down, viz.:—King, Queen, Prince of Wales, Duke of York, and Anson, besides two or three damaged in the same quarter. The walls of the mall and chapel remain entire. The fire was confined to the S. E. quarter."

High Admiral, on his presenting new colours to that distinguished corps.

In the several angles of the vestibule are casts from the colossal national statues in St. Paul's Cathedral, of our four principal naval heroes—Howe, St. Vincent, Duncan, and Nelson, having suspended over them flags, the trophies of their several victories, preserved, and until lately deposited, in St. Paul's Cathedral.

From the vestibule, a broad flight of steps lead to the saloon, or grand hall, 112 feet in length, and 56 in breadth (or a double cube), and 50 in height, ornamented with a range of Corinthian pilasters, standing on a basement, and supporting an entablature.

In the frieze around the hall is a Latin inscription, communicating the objects for which the Hospital was founded; and over the great arch at the upper end are the British arms, supported by two finely sculptured figures of *Mars* and *Minerva*.

The painted ceiling is described by Sir Richard Steele in the following words:—

"In the middle of the ceiling is a very large oval frame, painted in imitation of carved gold, with a great thickness rising in the inside, to throw up the figures to the greater height: the oval is fastened to a great suffite, adorned with roses, in imitation of copper. The whole is supported by eight gigantic figures of slaves, four on each side, as though they were carved in stone. Between the figures, thrown in heaps into a covering, are all manner of maritime trophies, in metzo relievo, as anchors, cables, rudders, masts, sails, blocks, capitals,* sea-guns, sea-carriages, boats, pinnaces, oars, stretchers, colours, ensigns, pendants, drums, trumpets, bombs, mortars, small arms, grenades, powder barrels, fire-arrows, grappling irons, cross staves, quadrants, compasses, &c.,† all in stone colours, to give the greater beauty to the rest of the ceiling, which is more significant.

"About the oval in the inside, are placed the twelve signs of the Zodiac: the six northern signs, as Aries, Taurus, &c., are placed on the north side, and the six southern signs, as Libra, Scorpio, &c., are to the south, with three of them in a groupe, which compose one quarter of the year. The signs have their attitudes and their draperies varied, and adapted to the seasons they possess: as the cool, the blue, and the tender green, to the spring; the

---

* "Capitals."—There is some obscurity in this word, no such article appearing in the present day, either in the gunner's, boatswain's, or carpenter's charge.

† It is difficult to know what Sir Richard wishes to include by the &c. after the many kinds of "maritime trophies" enumerated.

yellow to the summer, and the red and flame colour to the dog days, and autumnal season; the white, and cold, to the winter: likewise the fruits and flowers of every season, as they succeed each other.

"In the middle of the oval are represented King William and Queen Mary, sitting on a throne, under a great pavilion, or purple canopy, attended by the four cardinal virtues; as Prudence, Temperance, Fortitude, and Justice.

"Over the Queen's head is Concord, with the Fasces; at her feet two doves, denoting mutual concord and innocent agreement; with Cupid holding the king's sceptre, while he is presenting Peace, with the lamb and olive branch, and Liberty, expressed by the Athenian cap, to Europe; who, laying her crowns at his feet, receives them with an air of respect and gratitude.* The king tramples Tyranny under his

---

* The above sentence is not more vaguely than incorrectly expressed. The following is submitted as conveying a clearer idea:—Over the Queen's head is Concord, with the fasces; at her feet two doves, denoting mutual concord and innocent agreement, with Cupid holding the King's sceptre. Peace, with her lambs, is presenting an olive branch to, or receiving one from, the royal pair, or rather the Queen; and on the opposite side is a female figure, as of Europe, who has laid a crown at the feet of the King, which *his Majesty* appears to be receiving with an air of respect and gratitude.

feet; which is expressed by a French personage, with his leaden crown falling off—his chains, yoke, and iron sword broken to pieces — cardinal's cap—triple crowned mitres, &c., tumbling down; and at one end of the oval is a figure of Fame descending, sounding forth the praises of the Royal pair.

"Just beneath is Time bringing Truth to light; near which is a figure of Architecture, holding a large drawing of part of the Hospital, with the cupola, and pointing up to the royal founders; attended by the little Genii of her art. Beneath her is Wisdom and Heroic Virtue; represented by Pallas, and Hercules: they are represented in the act of destroying Ambition, Envy, Covetousness, Detraction, Calumny, with the other vices, which seem to fall to the earth, the place of their more natural abode.

"Over the Royal Pavilion is shewn, at a great height, Apollo in his golden chariot, drawn by four white horses, attended by the Horæ—the morning dews falling before him—going his course; and from him the whole plafond, or ceiling, is enlightened.

"Each end of the ceiling is raised in perspective, with a balustrade, and elliptic arches, supported by groupes of stone figures, which form a gallery of the whole length of the Hall—in the middle of which gallery, as though on the stocks, is seen the tafferil of the Blenheim man of war, with all her port-holes open, &c.; to one side of which, is a figure of Victory flying with the spoils taken from the enemy, and putting them on board the English man of war. Before the ship, is a figure, representing the City of London, with the arms, sword, and cap of maintenance, supported by Thame and Isis, with other small rivers offering up their treasures to her: the River Tyne, pouring forth sacks of coals. In the gallery, on each side of the ship, are the Arts and Sciences that relate to navigation, with the great Archimedes, and many old philosophers consulting the compass, &c.

"At the other end, as you return out of the Hall, is a gallery in the same manner, in the middle of which is the stern of a beautiful galley, filled with Spanish trophies; under which is the Humber, with his pigs of lead—the Severn with the Avon falling into her—with other lesser rivers.

"In the north end of the gallery, is the famous Tycho Brahe, that noble Danish knight, and great ornament of his profession, and human nature. Near him is Copernicus, with his Pythagorean system in his hand; next to him is an old mathematician, holding a large table, and on it are described two principal figures of the incomparable Sir Isaac Newton, on which many extraordinary things in that art are built.

"On the other end of the gallery to the south, is our learned Mr. Flamstead, Reg. Astron. Profess., with his ingenious disciple Mr. Thomas Weston. In Mr. Flamstead's hand is a large scroll of paper, on which is drawn the great eclipse of the sun, that will happen in April 1715; near him is an old man with a pendulum, counting the seconds of time, as Mr. Flamstead makes his observations with his great mural arch, (circle) and tube, on the descent of the moon on the Severn, (which at certain times forms such a roll of the tides, as the sailors corruptly call the Higre, instead of the Eager, and is very dangerous to all ships n its way: this is also expressed by rivers tumbling down by the moon's influence into the Severn.) All the great rivers at each end of the Hall, have their proper product of fish issuing out of their vases.

"In the four great angles of the ceiling, which are over the arches of the galleries, are the four elements; as Fire, Air, Earth and Water, represented by Jupiter, Juno, Cybele, and Neptune, with their lesser deities accompanying, as Vulcan, Iris, the Fauni, Amphitrite, with all their proper attitudes, &c.

"The whole raises in the spectator the most lively

images of glory and victory, and cannot be beheld without much passion and emotion."*

The above work was undertaken by Sir James Thornhill, in 1708, and not completed until 1727. There is great reason for believing, however, that a principal part of the merit of this painting is due to an Italian artist named Andrea, in the employ of Sir James Thornhill; which opinion is in a great measure substantiated, by the bad taste, and worse skill, shown in the painting of Sir James's own portrait, which he has thought fit to introduce at the upper end of the Hall.

In 1823, the Hall was converted into a Naval National Gallery, for the reception of portraits of distinguished officers, and of pictures illustrative of naval battles; with which it is at this time nearly filled.

Many of the pictures are by the most celebrated

---

* The author deems no apology necessary for inserting the lengthened details of this magnificent work of art, by so good an authority; especially as the description is from the pen of one who, living at the time the picture was painting, no doubt watched it in its progress from the commencement, and must therefore be considered qualified to give an accurate account of the painter's meaning.

artists, and amongst those of greatest merit must be ranked Loutherbourg's 1st of June action; Arnold's Nile action, at the moment of the explosion of L'Orient; the death of Nelson, by W. Devis; and Lord Duncan receiving the sword of the Dutch Admiral, De Winter, at the victory of Camperdown, by S. Drummond. The portraits comprise those of most of our admirals, and of many others connected with the service.*

Adjoining the Governor's house, is the Council Room, used for the trial of offenders against the regulations of the Hospital, and as a reading room for the officers. It is hung with portraits of James Duke of York, King William III., Queen Mary, George Prince of Denmark, George II., George III., and Queen Charlotte.

In the ante-Council Room is a library for the officers, an astronomical clock, and many pictures of much interest; amongst which is a full length portrait of Robert Osbolston, Esq., who bequeathed to the Hospital the sum of 20,000*l.* There are also a

---

* The present admission fee to *this* National Gallery, is "threepence each person." It is hoped, that when the funds of the Hospital are sufficiently rich, this tax upon the public will be dispensed with.

series of small pictures, delineating the burning of
the "Luxembourg Galley" in 1727. Captain Boys,
afterwards Lieutenant Governor of the Hospital, was
the second mate of the vessel at the time of the
accident, and one of the few survivors of the catastrophe; and an account has been handed down by
him of the circumstances, which are so interesting,
and extraordinary, that they are subjoined.

"On the 23rd day of May 1727, we sailed from
Jamaica, and on Sunday the 25th day of June,
were in latitude 41. 45 N., and longitude 20. 30 E.,
when the galley was perceived to be on fire in the
lazaretto," (sick bay.) "It was occasioned by the
fatal curiosity of two black boys, who, willing to
know whether some liquor spilled on the deck was
rum, or water, put the candle to it, which rose into
a flame, and immediately communicated itself to the
barrel from whence the liquor had leaked. It had
burned some time before it was perceived, as the boys
were too much intimidated to discover it themselves.

"Having tried all possible means to extinguish the
fire in vain, we hoisted out the yawl, which was
soon filled with twenty-three men and boys, who
had jumped into her with the greatest eagerness.
The wind now blowing very fresh, and she running
seven knots and a half by the log, we expected every

moment to perish, as she was loaded within a streak and a half of her gunnel. We had not a morsel of victuals, nor a drop of liquor, no mast, no sail, no compass to direct our course, and above a hundred leagues from any land.

"We left sixteen men in the ship, who all perished in her. They endeavoured to hoist out the long boat, but before they could effect it, the flames reached the powder room, she blew up, and we saw her no more. A little before this, we could distinguish the first mate and the captain's cook, in the mizen top, every moment expecting the fate that awaited them. Having thus been eye witnesses of the miserable fate of our companions, we expected every moment to perish by the waves, or, if not by them, by hunger and thirst.

"On the two first days it blew and rained much, but the weather coming fair on the third day, viz. the 28th, as kind Providence had hitherto wonderfully preserved us, we began to contrive means how to make a sail, which we did in the following manner: we took to pieces three men's frocks, and a shirt, and with a sail-needle and twine, which we found in one of the black boys' pockets, we made shift to sew them together, which answered tolerably well. Finding in the sea a small stick, we woulded it to a piece of a broken blade of an oar, that we had in the boat, and made a yard of it, which we hoisted on an oar, with our garters for halyards, and sheets, &c. A thimble, which the fore-sheet of the boat used to be reeved through, served at the end of the oar or mast, to reeve the halyards.

"Knowing from our observations that Newfoundland bore about north, we steered as well as we could to the northward. We judged of our course by taking notice of the sun, and of the time of the day by the captain's watch. In the night, when we could see the north star, or any of the great Bear, we formed the knowledge of our course by them.

"We were in great hopes of seeing some ship or other, to take us up. The fourth or fifth night, a man, Thomas Craniford, and the boy that unhappily set the ship on fire, died, and, in the afternoon of the next day, three more men, all raving mad, and crying out miserably for water.

"The weather now proved so foggy, that it deprived us almost all day of the sight of the sun, and of the moon and stars by night. We used frequently to halloo as loud as we could, in hopes of being heard by some ship. In the day time our deluded fancies often imagined ships so plain to us, that we have hallooed out to them a long time before we have been undeceived; and in the night, by the same delusion, we thought we heard men talk, bells ring, dogs bark, cocks crow, &c., and have condemned the phantoms of our imagination (believing all to be real ships, men, &c.) for not answering, and taking us up. The seventh day we were reduced to twelve in number by death. The next night, the wind being about E. N. E. blew very hard, and the sea running high, we scudded right before it with our small sail about a third down, expecting every moment to be swallowed up by the waves.

"July 5th Mr. Guishnet died, and on the 6th died Mr. Steward, (son of Dr. Steward of Spanish Town, in Jamaica) and his servant, both passengers. In the afternoon we found a dead duck, which looked green, and not sweet; we ate it however, (not without thanks to the Almighty,) and it is impossible for any person, except in the like unhappy circumstances, to imagine how pleasant it was to our tastes at that time, which at another, would have been offensive both to our taste and smell.

"On the 7th day of July, at one in the afternoon, we saw land about six leagues off. At four o'clock another man died, whom we threw overboard to lighten the boat. Our number was then reduced to seven. We had often taken thick fog-banks for land, which as often had given us great joy and hopes, that vanished with them at the same time; but when we really saw the land, it appeared so different from what we had so often taken for it, that we wondered how we could be so mistaken, and it is absolutely impossible for any man, not in our circumstances, to form an idea of the joy and pleasure it gave us, when we were convinced of its reality. It gave us strength to row, which we had not for four days before, and must infallibly, most of us, if not all, have perished that very night, if we had not got on shore: our souls exulted with joy and praises to our Almighty Preserver.

" About six o'clock we saw several shallops fishing, which we steered for. Having a fine gale of wind right on shore, we went, with sails and oars, about three or four knots; when we came so near that we thought one of the shallops could hear us (being just under sail, and going in with their fish,) we halloed as loud as we could; at length they heard us, and lowered their sail. When we approached pretty near them they hoisted it up again, and were going away from us, but we made so dismal and melancholy a noise that they brought to and took us in tow. They told us that our aspects were so dreadful that they were frightened at us. They gave us some bread and water; we chewed the bread small with our teeth, and then by mixing water with it, got it down with difficulty.

"During our voyage in the boat, our mouths had been so dry for want of moisture for several days, that we were obliged to wash them with salt water every two or three hours, to prevent our lips glueing fast together. In foggy weather, the sail having imbibed some moisture, we used to wring it into a pewter basin, which we found in the boat. Having wrung it as dry as we could, we sucked it all over, and used to lick one another's clothes with our tongues. At length we were obliged, by inexpressible hunger and thirst, to eat part of the bodies of six men, and drink the blood of four; for we had not, since we came from the ship, saved only one time about half a pint, and at another about a wine-glassful of water, each man, in our hats. A little food sufficing us, and finding the flesh very disagreeable, we confined ourselves to the hearts only.

"Finding ourselves now perishing with thirst, we were reduced to the melancholy, distressful, and horrid act of cutting the throats of our companions an hour or two after they were dead, to procure their blood, which we caught in a pewter basin, each man producing about a quart. But let it be remembered, in our defence, that without the assistance this blood afforded to nature, it was not possible that we could have survived to this time.

"At about eight o'clock at night we got on shore at Old St. Lawrence harbour, in Newfoundland, where we were kindly received by Captain Lecrass, of Guernsey or Jersey, then admiral of the harbour. We were cautioned to eat and drink but little at first, which we observed as well as the infirmity of human nature, so nearly starving, would allow. We could sleep but little, the transports of our joy being too great to admit of it. Our Captain, who had been speechless thirty-six hours, died about five o'clock the next morning, and was buried with all the honours that could be conferred upon him at that place.

"The boat in which we got to Newfoundland, a distance of 100 leagues, was only 16 feet long, 5 feet 3 inches broad, and 2 feet 3 inches deep. It was built for the Luxembourg galley by Mr. Bradley of Deal."

Lieutenant-Governor Boys rigidly spent the anniversaries of the days passed in the boat, in prayer and fasting, in commemoration of his providential deliverance.

REVENUE.

The revenues of the Hospital are derivable from various sources; and independent of Parliament, with the exception of an annual grant of 20,000*l.*, in lieu of merchant-seamen's sixpences. The duty of sixpence per man per month, on all mariners, was granted to the Hospital on the passing of the Register Act for Seamen in 1696.

In 1699, the following fines, levied against the undermentioned merchants for smuggling, amounting in all to 19,500*l.*, were added to the funds for building the Hospital, viz.:—John Gaudet, 1,500*l.*; David Barrow, 500*l.*; Stephen Seignoret, 10,000*l.*; Nicholas Santini, 1,500*l.*; Peter Dihane, 1,000*l.*; John Dumaitre, 1,000*l.*; —— Baudevin, 3,000*l.*

In 1705, Queen Anne made over to the Hospital 6,472*l.* 1*s.*, the proceeds of the effects of Captain Kidd, the noted buccaneer and pirate.

In 1708, by an act of Queen Anne's, the forfeited and unclaimed shares of prize and bounty money were given; and in 1710, 6,000*l.* per annum, out of the coal and culm tax, levied for building churches, was granted towards completing the Hospital and Chapel.

In 1735, by direction of his Majesty George II.,

the rents and profits of the forfeited estates of the decapitated Earl of Derwentwater were made over to the Hospital in perpetuity. As this property included various lead mines, the receipts were subject to great fluctuations; their average annual value may now be between 30,000*l.* and 40,000*l.* Annuities have, however, from time to time been granted to the descendants of the unfortunate Earl, out of the receipts.

Among the private donors, of which there are a great many on record, the most conspicuous is Robert Osbolston, Esq., who bequeathed property to the value of 40,000*l.*, to be equally divided between Greenwich Hospital and the Corporation of the Governors of Queen Anne's Bounty, for augmenting the small livings of the clergy. The property in question included the North and South Foreland light-houses, and the unexpired term of the grant of the dues. This grant was afterwards renewed for ninety-three years, and produced to the Hospital 7,000*l.* per annum; but on its expiration in 1832, these light-houses were transferred to the Trinity Board; the Hospital receiving no compensation for the loss of revenue.

From the above-mentioned sources, the Hospital is at present in possession of landed property of great value, and funded property to a large amount;

also of the revenues derived from property purchased in Greenwich, and from one-fourth per cent. on treasure shipped as freight in king's ships:—in all, varying from 130,000*l.* to 140,000*l.* per annum. This sum is barely sufficient for the maintenance of the four thousand persons attached to it,* and for keeping up, in its primitive splendour, the magnificent building.

ESTABLISHMENT.

The number of pensioners borne on the books of the establishment must not exceed 2,710; the vacancies are filled up every fortnight by the Admiralty, and as the candidates are numerous, the number is rarely much below the complement.† They are admitted, (marines and sailors indiscriminately), on account of their naval claims, whether arising from wounds received in action, or accidentally, or per-

---

* To give some idea of the expense incurred by the Hospital for provisions alone, for the 2710 pensioners on its books, I have made a calculation of the quantity of butcher's meat, (or money paid in lieu,) supplied annually, and find it exceeds 3035 sheep, of sixteen stone; and 867 oxen, of four cwt. each.

† The first pensioner, named John Worley, was admitted to the Hospital in 1704. A painting of him is preserved in the Painted Hall.

manent sickness contracted in the service, or good servitude, and old age.

There are 105 nurses, widows of seamen or marines, who are also selected by the Admiralty.

The military branch consists of a governor, lieutenant-governor, four captains, eight lieutenants, and two chaplains. There are also four matrons connected with the Hospital, widows of commissioned officers. The medical staff comprises a physician, surgeon, dispenser, and six assistants.

The civil establishment includes three paid commissioners, a secretary, steward, cashier, clerk of the cheque, architect, and clerk of the works, together with their clerks; whose duty it is to attend to the collection of the revenues, and all disbursements, receipts, and issues of stores, clothing, victualling, &c., which an establishment so extensive naturally gives rise to.

The pensioners are supplied with every necessary article of clothing and provisions, and have a weekly allowance of one shilling. There are 130 rated boatswains to take charge of the wards. These are selected from among the pensioners, and receive eighteenpence additional, or half-a-crown per week. Also nearly double the above number rated mates, who receive sixpence a week more than the private pensioners.

The clothing of the boatswains and mates are distinguished, the boatswains by broad gold lace, the mates by narrow lace, on their coats and hats.

The nurses are clothed in blue stuff gowns, with straw bonnets and blue ribbons, and a grey cloak. Their pay varies according to the duties they have to perform; those employed in the infirmary and helpless wards receiving nearly double what those in the building receive.

The following table will show in what manner the pensioners are distributed throughout the building :—

Table, shewing the Names of the Wards, with the Number of Men lodged in each.

Names of the Wards.	Number of Beds.	Names of the Wards.	Number of Beds.	Names of the Wards.	Number of Beds.
King Charles' Quarter—contains,		*Queen Anne's Quarter—*(cont.)		*King William's Quarter—*(cont.)	
Restoration	8	Princess Caroline	15	Namur	50
Royal Charles	37	Princess Mary	15	Union	48
London	12	Hamilton	15		
Neptune	12	Wager	16	Also, the Painted Hall, and four suites of Apartments.	516
Crown	35	Anson	16		
Saumarez	26	Barrington	19		
Royal Escape	6	Edinburgh	12		
Hardy	12	Victory	17	*Queen Mary's Quarter—contains,*	
Sandwich	12	Vanguard	24		
Coronation	52	Royal George	19	Rodney*	84
Nelson	36	St. Vincent	22	Council*	52
Melville	52	Royal Oak	24	Royal Charlotte	200
Lord Hood	32	Torrington	30	Prince of Wales	82
Prince	52	Cumberland	30	Jennings	72
Monk	52	Shrewsbury	17	Duke	128
Keats	12			Townsend	72
Association	16	And Apartments for 3 Captains, 3 Lieutenants, Chaplain, 2 Commissioners, the Cashier, and Clerk of the Cheque.	434	Queen	200
Palliser	48			Exmouth	72
				Clarence	96
Also, Apartments for the Governor, Lieutenant-Governor, Chaplain, and two Lieutenants.	512			Duke of York	34
				Also, the Chapel, and two suites of Apartments.	1092
		King William's Quarter—contains,			
Queen Anne's Quarter—contains,		Boyne*	44	ABSTRACT.	
		Nassau*	56	King Chas. Buildings	512
Windsor Castle	16	Adelaide	50	Queen Anne's do.	434
Augusta	18	Royal William	56	King William's do.	516
Howe	14	Ramillies	49	Queen Mary's do.	1092
Hawk	14	Barfleur	58		
Prince of Orange	17	Britannia	49	Total number of Beds	2554
Princess of Orange	15	Marlborough	56		
Norris	15				
Duncan	17				
Princess Amelia	15	* Wards for helpless men.		* Helpless Wards.	

The refectories are spacious halls, known as East, West, and South, and are underneath the Chapel, Painted Hall, and Western Colonnade; one (the East) containing eight hundred, another (the West) six hundred, and the third three hundred men.

Of the thousand men not accounted for, five hundred receive a money-allowance in lieu of their rations. Between two and three hundred are so infirm as to be unable to attend the halls, and they have their provisions taken to them by nurses and helpers hired for the purpose of attending them. A great many are in different lunatic asylums, and a number equal to the remainder in the Infirmary.

At the upper end of the West Dining Hall is a cast from a correctly executed marble bust of the late Governor, Admiral Sir Richard Keats, by Behnes, which was presented to his late Majesty by the Admiral's widow. Under it is the following inscription :—

Admiral
SIR RICHARD GOODWIN KEATS, G.C.B.
Governor of Greenwich Hospital,
A.D. MDCCCXXXII.
A testimony of personal respect
From the Military and Civil Officers
Of the Hospital,
and
In commemoration
Of the benevolence that devised,
And zeal that accomplished,
The improved system of victualling
The Pensiouers.

Under which is the crest and motto :—Mi patria es mi norti.

The following Tables of diet will give the reader an idea of the improvement alluded to in the foregoing inscription.

TABLE OF DIET PREVIOUS TO THE CHANGE.

Days.	Bread loaves of 16 oz.	Beer qts.*	Beef lbs.	Mutton lbs.	Butter oz.	Cheese lbs.	Pease pints.
Sunday....	1	2	0	1	0	1/4	0
Monday....	1	2	1	0	0	1/4	0
Tuesday....	1	2	0	1	0	1/4	0
Wednesday	1	2	0	0	1	1/2	1/2
Thursday...	1	2	1	0	0	1/4	0
Friday....	1	2	0	0	1	1/2	1/2
Saturday...	1	2	1	0	0	1/4	0
Total per week.	7	14	3	2	2	2 1/4	1

PRESENT SCALE.

Days.	Bread lbs.	Beer pints†	Beef lbs.	Mutton lbs.	Butter oz.	Morning Chocolate Mk. & Sugar, pints	Evng. Tea, do. pints	Potatoes, or 1/2 lb of bread extra.
Sunday....	1	3	0	1	1/2	1	1	1/2
Monday....	1	3	1/2	0	1/2	1	1	1/2
Tuesday....	1	3	0	3/4	1/2	1	1	1/2
Wednesday	1	3	3/4	0	1/2	1	1	1/2
Thursday...	1	3	0	3/4	1/2	1	1	1/2
Friday....	1	3	3/4	0	1/2	1	1	1/2
Saturday...	1	3	0	3/4	1/2	1	1	1/2
Total per week.	7	21	2 1/4	3 1/4	3 1/2	7	7	3 1/2

* Old Measure. † Imperial Measure.

That the spirit of Greenwich Hospital does not confine itself to the bodily wants of the pensioners, to the exclusion of mental necessities, is evidenced by the very excellent library, selected by a highly talented gentleman holding a responsible situation in the Hospital, and purchased for their exclusive use by the institution. Their reading-room is fifty feet in length, heated by two large fires, and furnished with oaken tables, benches, and chairs, for their accommodation. It contains 1440 volumes, comprising a most complete library of voyages, travels, and naval history, together with a little of politics, magazines from 1740, encyclopedia, and many popular and amusing novels; also the Atlas, Record, Portsmouth paper, and Navy List. The books are all well bound, and stamped on the covers with the Hospital arms.

The walls are hung round with a complete set of Carey's maps, framed; there are also provided two twenty-four-inch globes, terrestrial and celestial.

On one side of the room, in the centre, is a marble bust of Dibdin, the naval bard, presented by the patriotic fund. The whole is designed and executed with much feeling; and on the tablet beneath are the following lines, from his own "Tom Bowling," inscribed as his epitaph:—

> "And though his body's under hatches,
> His soul is gone aloft."

It is to be regretted that so few of the pensioners avail themselves of the privileges thus extended to them; not more than twenty or thirty using the library.

INFIRMARY.

The Infirmary is a quadrangular brick building, without ornaments, 198 feet in length, and 175 in breadth, three stories high, and capable of accommodating from 300 to 400 patients, with most of the medical officers. It was commenced in 1763, and has been constructed with the strictest regard to the comforts and wants of its inmates.

48   ACCOUNT OF

The following Tables are interesting, as showing the Mortality amongst the Pensioners at the present day, as compared with that fifty years back.

COMPLEMENT, 2350.

YEARS.	JAN.	FEB.	MARCH.	APRIL.	MAY.	JUNE.	JULY.	AUGUST.	SEPT.	OCT.	NOV.	DEC.	Total in the year.
1777	18	13	15	13	11	18	11	15	19	16	21	15	185
1778	18	11	11	22	16	19	11	19	16	16	21	14	194
1779	19	18	25	22	16	13	16	15	19	19	15	18	215
1780	30	19	17	21	15	17	15	13	17	25	15	20	224
1781	14	15	16	18	22	11	15	18	16	23	15	23	206
1782	16	19	15	21	24	31	18	16	16	16	17	19	228
1783	18	15	17	14	12	17	13	15	16	17	15	19	188
1784	17	25	21	25	22	14	13	6	6	10	10	17	186
1785	20	16	14	16	14	18	21	19	15	15	10	17	195
1786	11	20	20	12	13	20	8	18	15	7	24	8	176
1787	36	14	12	20	11	16	14	11	14	16	27	21	212
1788	13	15	22	20	13	11	16	15	15	14	12	25	191
in each mth.	230	200	205	224	189	205	171	180	184	194	202	216	2400

COMPLEMENT, 2710.

	JAN.	FEB.	MARCH.	APRIL.	MAY.	JUNE.	JULY.	AUGUST.	SEPT.	OCT.	NOV.	DEC.	Total
1825	33	17	19	15	20	18	21	19	14	16	26	17	233
1826	38	19	14	16	20	21	21	16	22	33	17	19	246
1827	25	23	20	24	25	15	17	14	28	24	16	22	253
1828	17	24	18	26	19	23	20	22	21	27	26	13	256
1829	23	26	25	17	18	18	16	20	15	21	22	22	243
1830	40	25	21	18	17	20	15	19	19	15	22	14	245
1831	33	27	31	20	46	37	17	31	19	20	18	20	289
1832	20	25	23	19	21	24	23	20	20	14	25	20	254
1833	22	25	31	32	26	18	22	35	22	21	11	20	285
1834	20	28	18	15	19	16	20	39	26	24	21	27	273
1835	35	30	35	20	28	29	17	20	25	20	23	22	304
1836	27	18	28	21	23	29	17	18	26	16	19	17	259
in each mth.	323	287	283	243	252	268	226	273	257	251	246	233	3142

Making a comparative average increase of thirty deaths in the year. It must, however, be observed that, in most cases, the men are much older when admitted than was formerly the custom.

SCHOOLS.

The schools of the Royal Hospital are separated by the main road, called Romney-road, from its having formerly belonged to the Earl of Romney, who bequeathed it, with other property in Greenwich, to the Hospital.

The schools are divided into the Upper School, Lower School for boys, and Lower School for girls.

The Upper School consists of four hundred boys, one hundred of whom are the sons of Commissioned, or Ward-room Warrant Officers, and are nominated by the First Lord of the Admiralty; the remaining three hundred are children of officers, or seamen, or marines in the Navy, or Merchant Service, and are presented by fourteen patrons. The boys of this school are much famed for their mathematical knowledge: they are for the most part sent into the Merchant Service, which they have materially served to extricate from the stigma, some years back attached to it, namely, that of being the worst navigated of any ships in the civilized world.

The Lower School for boys contains four hundred, sons of seamen or marines of the Royal Navy. They are admitted entirely on account of the claims of the father on the service, no interest being suffered to influence their selection. The Lower Schoolboys are not taught navigation, but made to learn trades. The same description applies to the Girls' School, which consists of two hundred.

When we reflect on the vast utility of Greenwich Hospital, the large number it supports, and the liberal spirit in which its bounties are bestowed, we feel that we are contemplating something noble, and are sure that the country wherein rests the generous sympathies which stimulated its foundation, and gave vigour to its growth, will ever maintain its present elevated state, amidst surrounding nations. It was the spirit which actuated our gallant heroes in fighting their country's battles, that led to the creation of Greenwich Hospital, and the desire of adding to its renown; and so long as this noble pile rears its lofty head to the skies, so long will it remain a convincing proof, that England's sons are not less generous than they are brave!

THE GREENWICH PENSIONERS.

CHAPTER I.

> "What tho' on hamely fare we dine,
>   Wear hoddin grey, and a' that;
> Gie fools their silks, and knaves their wine,
>   A man 's a man for a' that.
>   For a' that, and a' that,
>   Their tinsel show, and a' that;
>   The honest man, tho' e'er sae poor,
>   Is king o' men for a' that."—BURNS.

FOUR times in the course of the year, "Greenwich pensioners" have two very strong and almost irresistible inducements to make themselves merry. One is, they are supplied with an extra good dinner—consisting of a pound each of corned pork, with excellent pea-soup, and two quarts of strong ale; and the other, the absence of punishment for any minor offences they may commit. These are privileged days, called festivals, and are held on their Majesties' birth-days,* coronation day, and on the anniversary of the landing of the royal founder, William III., at Torbay,—who, together with his royal consort Mary, endowed Greenwich Hospital with its charter.

It is the custom, in the mornings of these days, to muster all the pensioners in their best clothes, to form them round the Grand Square, and then, the officers accompanying in full uniform, to march them into the chapel to prayers: the boys of the upper school, carrying globes, quadrants, &c., preceding.

After divine service, the officers and boys cross over from the Chapel to the Painted Hall, where a certain set of loyal toasts are given out, and drank by the officers; to each of which the boys reply, with three deafening cheers.

---

* The periods will of course be altered to suit the present reign; but *four* days will still be set apart for festivals.

On these festive occasions, an universal smile pervades the whole race—nothing like discontent is to be seen on their brows—" their spirits shine through them;" and I have chosen one of them, as the best adapted to my purpose. But in order to obtain a more than casual glimpse of these interesting beings, it is necessary to folow them to their wards; to one of which it is my wish and intention to conduct the attention of the indulgent reader.

This ward, which bears the name of a great naval hero, is a very comfortable, commodious long room, measuring about sixty feet by twenty. On each side are ranges of cabins, about seven feet square, for the use of fifteen men (the full complement); a space of ten feet on one side, in the middle of the ward, being left for the fire-place. The windows look into Queen Anne's Square. This ward is considered one of the most comfortable in the building; and as it is desirable to show these veterans in their best aspect, it is purposely selected.

Over the lofty mantel-piece is fixed a wooden clock, originally purchased by subscription among the ward inmates, with the understanding that it should revert to the longest liver of the then race of occupants. It is rather a troublesome piece of furniture; for all the regulating hitherto used has been ineffectual towards making it keep time.

Another piece of furniture, subject to the same conditions, is a pembroke mahogany table, at present decorated with various drinking vessels. Long stools are ranged on each side of this table, in the snug nook formed by the jutting bulk-heads of the cabins on either side of the fire-place.

The table is covered—(a mark of refinement quite unexpected)—with a piece of green baize, not *much* the dirtier for wear. There are on it two yellow basins, one tin pannikin, a glass— the stem of which having been broken, by dint of patience and a hard stone, it has been again made useful—and two half-gallon stone beer-bottles.

The present festival is " Founders'-day,"— Nov. 4. It is now 3 h. 30 m. P.M., and the effects of the " long pull," and the " strong pull," are beginning to make themselves visible.

The day being rather cold, and, as a November day always is, miserable, the fire which blazes so cheerfully in the large old-fashioned fire-place adds an inexpressible degree of comfort to the company around it, whom, without any further prelude, I will bring before the reader.

Near the fire-place on the left hand (for I like to go with the sun)—that is, supposing yourself to be standing with your back to the fire—is Tim Stuart.

Tim Stuart is, I should think, not far from seventy years of age. He has but one available eye; the place of the other, if not entirely untenanted, being covered with a black silk shade. His hair is quite white, very long, and combed back with great care over his poll. He has been tolerably good looking; his nose is well formed, his remaining eye large and piercing, and his skull as finely shaped as the warmest disciple of Gall and Spurzheim would desire. His height may be five feet nine, and his figure well proportioned.

Unfortunately, Tim has acquired so great a relish for grog, that it has procured him, with some, the character of a drunkard; that is, he is one of those who, when they have been drinking, allow every one to know it by becoming quarrelsome. A proof of his imprudence is at hand: a week ago, he was foolish enough to barter his allowance of ale for a glass of grog, for which he is now doing penance. As may be supposed, he is an exception to the general rule—he is a cup too low; and reminds one forcibly of Falstaff's description of himself under similar circumstances, when he says he is " as melancholy as a lugged bear." His case is certainly a deplorable one, for not one of his wardmates have the charity to spare him a single drop.

Beside him is a man with a face like a hatchet, and a body as thin as its handle, called Fat Jack. His proper name is William Brown; but his customary title being Fat Jack, for the sake of distinction it will be better to use it. The name was originally conferred upon him by his opposite neighbour, who

happens to be quite as inappropriately named
—Dick Summers, *alias* Slender.

'' 'Dick,' or 'Slender,' as he is usually called,
in his shoes might measure five feet in height,
and appears to be nearly three feet in breadth.
There is nothing he more closely resembles in
figure, than his own two-quart stone beer-bottle;
which, I may mention, stands half empty before
him, and forms the subject of his cogitations.
Slender is " a fellow of infinite jest;" he is a
character which it will take some time to
develope, and is supposed to be fond of " drawing the long bow."

Tobias Williams, or ' Toby,' completes the
assembled company. Toby has taken up his
winter-quarters in the corner nearest the fire,
from which he rarely emerges, except to get
his meals, and to go to his cabin. He is at
present in a state of lethargy bordering on a
nod; but as his ale-bottle requires his protection, he restrains himself. Toby has a large
red nose; for which cause he is sometimes
called ' Nosey.' Its present aspect is most
fiery. He is one of the few men left who sport

tails; and when we consider the many perils it must have encountered, its preservation is little short of miraculous.

Tim was very thirsty, and might have remained so, had it not been for Toby, who, requiring a *chaw*—(there is no other word sufficiently expressive)—and having neither tobacco, money, nor credit, was glad to negotiate with Tim, who chanced to have a stock on hand.

This affair being settled to their mutual satisfaction, each relapsed into his former state; from which they were soon aroused by hearing —thump—thump—thump along the ward floor, announcing the arrival of Thomas Peters.

As Peters is doomed to occupy a great many of the succeeding pages, it is necessary to be more particular in his description. He is moderately all, rather thin, about sixty years of age, and has lost his right leg. His exterior shows at once that he is not in his right place; for although attired in the coat of the pensioner, you may discover about him a certain something, which denotes him to have been at one time a gentleman.

There are times when deep sorrow seems to overwhelm him; and when these moments come over him, he seems to resort to the happiness of others for relief. He never seems more pleased than when surrounded by the odd characters in the ward, and as he appears not to want money, he is continually doing his utmost to make them merry.

There is a degree of eccentricity about Peters, which cannot well be accounted for; but if the reader has patience to follow me, it is intended to elucidate the mystery, as far as his history will do so.

"Hurrah, my lads! cheer up!" said he, advancing: "look at that," at the same time throwing a five-shilling piece on the table. They simultaneously started up in amazement and delight.

"A crown, by the pipers!" exclaimed the enraptured Tim, shaking off the blues with astonishing rapidity.

"Why, who have you been plundering again?" asked Fat Jack.

"It warms one's heart to look at it," said Slender; verifying his remark by offering poor Tim a swig at the ale bottle.

Toby was also moved with delight: his nose itched, as it always did on those occasions; and he gave vent to his extreme satisfaction by a significant grunt.

"Now, who is to go and get a bottle of rum?" said Peters.

"I'll go," said Old Tim, coming forward.

"That you won't," replied Peters. "You remember how you served me the last time—don't you?—when I gave you three shillings to get some grog, you made a start, and we didn't see you for a whole week, and then the devil a coat had you to your back. No, no,—my Old Tim; I don't mean to trust *you* with a five-shilling piece—I have too much regard for you."

"Well, as you like," muttered Tim, disappointed. "I own I made a 'slip bend' that time; but I couldn't help it. I met an ould messmate that I hadn't seen for twenty year, and if I'd been sure of a hanging I wouldn't have parted company 'athout giving him a glass of grog."

A new comer relieved them at once of the difficulty. It was no other than Jerry Jones, the mate of the ward; who deserves more than a passing remark. Had Jerry lived in Steele's days, he would have been received *nem. con.* as a distinguished member of the " Ugly Club;" and at the present day it would be safe to back him against the whole county, at grinning through a horse collar.

In the first place, he is very short, and his legs assume the figure of a pair of closed callipers; his toes meeting and overcasting each other considerably as he walks. On his back, or rather his right shoulder, is something approaching closely to a hump; and the left is depressed in proportion to the elevation of the right: in a word, his shape sets all rules of symmetry at defiance. But the most remarkable of all is his face. It is very long, and much marked with the small-pox; added to which, his small grey eyes never seem to co-operate; for as surely as one looks to the right, the other is directed straight forward; and I never saw the comical effect equalled by any set of features except Liston's. His nose, originally of the *snub* kind, has been much disturbed by coming in contact with a post—(no doubt through his not rightly allowing for the angular defect in his organs of vision); and so much has the collision affected this feature, that it has ever since pointed dejectedly to his right shoulder. His mouth strongly resembles that of a codfish.

Jerry is a good-natured fellow, and a great favourite. He is so much used to witticisms on his person, that he can join as heartily as the punster in the laugh raised at his expense. Jerry is married too; most ugly men are; probably because they are determined the world shall not think them too ill-looking to captivate.

"Here comes Jerry," was the exclamation; "he will go in a twinkling."

"Ullo, shipmates," said Jerry, in a strong nasal twang, caused by the displacement of his nose, but which did not conceal the fact of his being a native of the Great Metropolis; advancing with his usual waddle to the table: "what's in the wind now?—got any ale to spare?—it's wery poor stuff. to-day."

"Uh, uh," grunted Old Toby (Jerry's unsuccessful rival at drinking beer—for Jerry's head was as hard as a stone, and he was never known to be drunk), "you're there, are you! what have you done with your own?"

"Done wi' it, my old Nosey!" said Jerry, "Vy, took it home to missus, to be sure; don't you think the old gal likes it as vell as me?" This answer was followed by a loud laugh; they all knowing the small portion which had fallen to the "old *gal's*" lot.

"And now," continued Jerry, unheeding the laughter, "I'm come to look after the vard, and keep you—you old grog-tub—from tumbling into the fire."

"Well, here's something for you to do, my little Cupid," said Peters. "Take this"—giving him the five-shilling piece—"and go to Muckle's for a bottle of rum, and then to old Sal Morrison's for some pipes and tobacco; and take care," added he, " to let me see your handsome face again in less than ten minutes—or, mark me, I'll put that nose of yours on the other tack for you. Now, away you go, and remember I always keep my word."

Admonished by this speech, Jerry made his reappearance three minutes within the given time, laden with a bottle of rum, half-a-dozen pipes, and a large paper of tobacco. "And there's your change, Mr. Tom," said he, depositing his cargo, " and see it's all right. But how shall we manage about smoking in the vard: you know it's quite contrary to orders; and old Harry" (the boatswain of the ward) " vill be coming in malty presently, and kick up a row 'bout it, and then I shall ' lose my lace'* for allowing of it."

" Don't be alarmed about him," said Slender; " there he lies in the bottom of his cabin hard and fast for the next watch; he soon finished his two quarts."

---

* Be reduced to a private pensioner by being disrated.

"Then," said Jerry, " we'll fasten his cabin door, and keep him in, and turn to."

All were invited to partake: and now commences the sport. The cork is drawn, water in a large black jack, and pannikins, or basins, procured; the pipes lighted; and the jolly six draw near the table.

CHAPTER II.

"The bottle 's the sun of our table,
  His beams are rosy wine,
We—planets who are not able,
  Without his help to shine.
Let mirth and glee abound,
  You'll soon grow bright,
  With borrowed light.
And shine as he goes round!"

Drinking Song.

"Look at old Tim," said Slender; "see how he brightens up; he looked just now like Beachy Head in a fog; he is not the same man he was an hour ago." Indeed, the whole party were in an instant united by the creative power of grog.

A glass of grog is sure to cast loose a sailor's tongue; and you will observe him thaw like ice before the fire, as that generous, though much abused beverage, mounts to his brain.

"Is it true what I heard t'other day," said old Tim, "that they don't mean to sarve out any more grog board a man-of-war?"

"Nonsense," replied Peters, — "they may just as well not supply any more powder and shot. Grog is ammunition for our insides as much as powder and shot for the cannon's; and it is only the over-charging that does the mischief. Wer'n't you at the Nile, Tim?" asked the President, turning to a more interesting subject—(for, seated in a large arm-chair, Peters did the honours, as well as give the feast).

"Yes, to be sure I was," replied Tim, bridling up; "and had a double whack of fighting, but not of prize-money. I was in the old Leander. Ah!" said the old fellow, with much feeling—brought out, no doubt by the magician 'grog'—"and never, while this old hulk keeps afloat, shall I forget that noble ship."

"Not so noble either,"- returned Peters. "She was only one of the old fifties."

"That's true," said Tim; "but didn't she take the station of a line-of-battle ship at the Nile, and we *all but* took one of the biggest seventy-fours in the French navy?"

"What, the Genereux, you mean, I suppose, that took you," rejoined Peters.

"You may call her *Jinnyroo*, if you likes, but I can read a little, and her right name is the *Generux*, if I knows anything about it," urged Tim, authoritatively.

"To be sure it is," said Fat Jack. "'Sides, I don't care to speak like a Frenchman; if I can speak my own mother tongue, it's quite enough for me."

"Well, *Generux*, if you like it then," said Peters, "by all means; but how did you manage to get taken?"

"Taken!" said old Tim, starting up, and holding his pipe in the air—"Why, she was three to one against us. Why, we begun the action eighty men short of complement, and there wasn't less than eight or nine hundred men aboard of the Frenchman to fight our three hundred; and then look'ee, we had only long eighteens, and nines, to his thirty-sixes and eighteen pounders. Ah! if all our chaps had been aboard, she wouldn't have had the old Leander to tow after her.

"You see," continued old Tim, still standing up, "we got out of the Nile action better off than ere a ship there; for our Captain was a brave and good officer, and looked out a snug berth for us, just under the bows of a big eighty-gun ship, so that they could only give us their bow guns in exchange for our broadside; and we play'd Old Scratch with 'em. Rest his soul! he was a taught hand; but give me that afore one of your milk-and-water, grog-stopping, leave-stopping, black-list fellows, as torments a man for a month or two. If a man gets drunk when he ought to be sober, why let him take his whack, and have done with it. ¶ often goes and peeps in through the railings, at the *moniment* in the *Moloncholy*,* and thinks to myself,

---

* The Hospital cemetery (so called), where a handsome pillar, representing a flag lowered, is erected to the memory of this gallant officer,—Sir T. B. Thomson,—once treasurer of the Hospital.

sometimes—he might have had worse anchoring ground than along with his old shipmates."

"But go on with the battle," said Peters, "because I don't see there's any *disgrace* in being beaten, when the enemy is so much stronger."

"Disgrace!" repeated old Tim, with energy. "I've fought in two general actions, and was at the cutting out of the '*Le Desiry*,' from Dunkirk, when I belonged to the Dart—that wasn't amiss neither—and in plenty of other work; but, I can tell you, I'm not so proud of my Trafalgar medal,* as of that fight in the old Leander. —Disgrace!" re-echoed the old man, who didn't like the word at all—" I considers as every man in the ship done his duty like he ought, though we did get taken."

"Well, I meant no harm," replied Peters, a little disconcerted.

"No, no," said old Tim, "I know you didn't;

---

* What can be a greater slur on the country, than the fact, that the only medals which the brave seamen, who fought so nobly in that action, were presented with, were given by a private individual; and then only to a few?

give us your flipper, my old boy; I know you for a noble heart, and one as ought to be a Post-Captain, 'stead of an old College-man, if right come to right." Saying which, he gave poor Tom's hand a squeeze, which, if the sentiment did not, brought tears to his eyes.

"Come, old boy," said Peters, "sit down, and tell us all about that business. I know it's a credit to all of you for holding out like you did: I only said that to draw you along."

Tim accordingly resumed his seat, and, after relighting his pipe, and puffing a cloud which wafted its way to the lofty ceiling, was going to commence his yarn, when a fresh visiter arrived, and a very welcome one, named Jim Roberts; who made himself doubly welcome by another bottle of rum: he seated himself, and old Tim commenced his story after the following manner:—

"After the Nile action, you know, our ship being ready for another, we was ordered to carry the account of the action to the Admiral of the station; and Captain Berry, that's Lord Nelson's Flag-Captain, was sent on board with the despatches, for a passage. Just eighteen days after the action, at daybreak in the morning, we was lying becalmed under the Island of 'Candy,' and we see a large ship standing towards us with a light breeze.

"We soon made her out to be one of the Nile ships, 'cause of the white patches over the shotholes, 'bout her bows, and 'cordingly cleared for action. You see, 'twas quite impossible like, for us to get away if we tried, 'cause the ship was land-locked.

"We didn't take long to clear for action: there was no fine looking-glasses, and *sofees*, and large *libaries*, in our Captains' cabins in them days; as one of our chaps, as was captain's-steward in a ship a little while ago, says there is now. Why, he wants to make me believe as there's as many books in some Captains' cabins as in our *libary** over the way—but it won't do. Hows'ever, we had no books but the Purser's,

---

* This library contains several hundred well-selected vols., entirely devoted to the use of the pensioners, as mentioned in the introduction.

in the old Leander, and I was never very deep in them.

"We piped to breakfast at one bell in the morning watch. I suppose our Captain thought as the Frenchmen wouldn't give us a bellyfull; be that as it may, we had nothin' but *geo-graffy*, that's cold water and biscuit, as you knows very well, and many a poor fellow never had another.

"We had matter of fifteen hands wounded lying in their hammocks, when we commenced the action, who got hurt at the Nile. Poor fellows! we lost near hand a hundred men, killed and wounded, afore we struck. Well, so soon as we'd done breakfast—not long first, you may be sure, when our enemy was in sight—the drum beat to quarters. Some of our crew said as how Captain Thomson wanted to run the ship ashore, to save the men's lives, only Captain Berry—a *reg'lar* fire-eater—wouldn't let him. But I don't believe it: our captain valued his name too much for that—though, for that matter, we might have got off better if he had. But there was no knowing till we tried, but what we might take him, and if we had not been short so many men, it's my belief she would have been our prize.

"I was doing quartermaster's duty at that time, though rather a young hand, and 'twas my watch on deck when we first made her out. When they beat to quarters after breakfast, I give up the wheel to the captain's coxen, and went to my quarters on the main-deck. About one bell in the forenoon watch, up came the Frenchman, blazing away, right and left, long afore he was in gun-shot, and wasting the powder and shot as we wanted.

"So when he come pretty close to us, the word passed to lie down at our quarters, to receive their broadside; and they began to hit us, but hurt no one. At last we had the word of command given us—'to fire.' And we give him as good as he sent. The Frenchman was close along-side, and all our guns, double-shotted. He then ran us aboard by the fore-chains, and tried to board, but they got off with the worst of it. Our division of boarders was called up from below, to lend a hand to keep them off, and one fellow struck the point of a boarding pike in my cheek,—you can only just see the mark. Poll said it spoil'd my face when she first saw me afterwards; but when she heard I was a *stager*, with plenty of money, she told me it made me look quite beautiful. —Ay," continued the old man, with a grin, " they'd tell Old Blueskin so, if he had lots of prize-money coming to him."

"*Steady*," said Peters.

"Steady," responded Tim, continuing his story. "Well, our mizen-mast was shot away, and a breeze come off the land, and the French ship shot a-head clear of us, and we managed to get a chance of raking her. We poured every shot of our broadside into her cabin windows, and sent many a *Johnny Crappo* to the bar of the other world. But it soon came to their turn, and they fired their whole broad-side into us, a thin pistol-shot. It shook us from stem to starn, and many a bold fellow lost the number of his mess.

"We fought six hours; just think of that. Why, if she had handled her guns in a seamanlike manner, she ought to have sunk us in little more than six minutes. We had to cut through the main-topsail, lying over our larboard side, to make room for the muzzles of the guns,—for our ship was quite a wreck—not a stick standing—but still the brave hearts wouldn't give in. Fore and aft there was no murmuring, every man was ready to stick by the craft till she sunk; and once, when she sheered off to repair damages, we gave three cheers, and turned-to, making cartridges, and refitting all we could to give chase. We fired every thing we could get hold of—crow-bars, nails, and all sorts, cause we had used all our shot. I saw one of the crow-bars sticking through her deck afterwards; and they never had a harder day's work in their lives than when they took the little Leander. We killed near three hundred of them, afore we surrendered. But we lost two Leftenants, the Master, the Boatswain, and a third part of the crew; and the great lubberly hulk had taken up his berth under our starn, to give us another broadside.

"So our brave Captain, thinking as we had

fought long enough, for it was now past five bells in the afternoon watch, ordered our colours to be hauled down,* and the old English ensign, all in strips, was struck; and the despatches, in three large bags, were thrown out of the cabin windows, with shot in them.

"As soon as the Frenchmen seed as how we had struck, one of their Midshipmen,—*haspirongs* they calls 'em—and two or three men, swam on board of us, (for neither had a boat that could swim;) they were stark naked, and they dived down below at once, and rigged themselves in any of our clothes they could get hold of: and not one of us offered to hinder them. At last the Frenchmen managed to mend one of their boats with tarpaulins, so as to get us aboard their ship. We had not many traps left us, to take away; for lots of the

---

* It has been said the Leander showed her submission by holding a French jack out upon a boarding pike. It will be seen Timothy differs from this account, and he, moreover, persists in it—that the colours remained up to the last. He being on the main-deck, might have a wrong idea, but is nevertheless, positive on the point.

Frenchmen soon swam aboard, and took care of our bags for us. Some of us thought it better to wear two shirts, but as soon as we got to the French ship, one of them was taken away.

"Captain *Jolly* was a great scoundrel, and used our Captain like a brute: his men in the Leander stole the Doctor's instruments, when he was going to dress the men's wounds, for the wounded men were all left aboard; and he (Captain Lejoille) 'kept him,' (the Doctor) from coming aboard the French ship to our Captain, who was badly wounded.

"We had not any thing but oil and rice to eat, and they made us work, and refit the ship. We fished his foremast, (another shot would have knocked it down,) and knotted all his shrouds; for which Captain Jolly promised us our liberty, as soon as we got to Corfu; but as soon as we had done all the work, he started us down below, and kept us close, till we got there. But, you see, we can't wonder at their being a little matter spiteful. See what a thrashing they got at the Nile, and you know we shouldn't have liked such a beating as that ourselves.

"Captain Jolly was one of your *Brittoon**
men, and could speak English as well as any of
us: he wanted to get some of our chaps to
enter for his ship, but not a man of us would
have done so to save their lives. He didn't
know much of our hearts, if he did of our language, if he thought to make any of us fight
against our country. One of our maintopmen
said to him, when he asked him to enter for the
ship, says he—'No, d——n your ship, and
service too; why, a French prisoner in England gets a better dinner every day than you
do, although you're Captain of this lubberly
craft.' He got in a terrible passion, and swore
he'd shoot him; but Ben Thompson cared little
for his threat—he wasn't the man to flinch.

"Well, when we got to Corfu, they sent us
ashore to a dirty prison, where they used us as
bad as they did in the ship; and it was two or

---

* Tim probably means a native of Brittany.

three months afore they sent some of us, and I among them, aboard a merchantman, bound to Trieste; but as soon as we got out, we rose upon the crew, and made them take us to Naples, where we at last arrived, with hardly a rag to cover us, and half starved."

" Bravo! old boy," shouted they all, " that's the best yarn you ever told yet."

" It's dry work, though," replied Tim; " so just pass the bottle this way, Mr. Tom, don't be keeping all the grog to yourself."

" Ay, that was a brave action," said Roberts, who had listened with the greatest attention to old Tim, " and none of you need be ashamed of such a defeat,—it was more credit to you than half the victories during the war."

"I was at the Nile too," said little Dick Slender, (who had, during Tim's tale, been making himself very busy with the grog bottle,) " and no ship in the action fought better, nor lost more men, than the old Swiftsure, or *Slow-and-Sure*, as some of us called her—that was Captain *Haulwell*."

" Now for it," interrupted Fat Jack—(Slender's mortal enemy at yarning)—"stand by, for when old Dick gets hold of the Nile, you may look out."

"Well, old Famine," retorted Slender, "if I do stretch a little, you're always at hand to tail on a fathom or two. But this I'm going to tell you is a downright"—

(Here he was unable to proceed, from a terrible fit of sneezing, caused by Fat Jack's slyly inserting a snuff-box under his nose.)

"Sneezer," said Famine, speaking to him.

"I'll pay you off for that, you old dried eel-skin," said Slender, as soon as he could fetch breath, "you know I'm not much in your debt in the long run."

"Come tell us that story, Dick," said Peters; "Fat Jack is only afraid you will cut him out."

"Why, as for the matter of that," replied Slender, "its well-known he's got up many a galley-packet. But this 'ere yarn is"—

"Let us hear it," said Peters, "and then we can judge of the truth."

"You all knows as how the Nile action begun at sunset; so it's no manner of sarvice my telling you that ; and our ship warn't the fastest in the fleet, and accordingly she didn't get into the action not till late. We could see the blaze, and steered right for it — our chaps warn't skulkers, as everybody knows, and the fault was the old *Slow-and-Sure's.* There was the Billyruffin just coming out with a right down skinfull, and we hailed 'em, but didn't get any answer, there was such a terrible noise aboard of her. At last we got into the thick of it, and let go the anchor right alongside of one of the French line. Soon as that was done there was ' Furl sails' "——

" Hold on there," interrupted Peters—"you surely didn't furl sails in the heat of the action."

" Why," said Dick pettishly, " how could this 'ere thing have come to pass if we hadn't ? Just let me alone, will you. You see I was captain of the maintop then."

" You mean the *mizen* top, I think," said Peters.

" I wish you'd let me go on, Mr. Tom," returned Slender, rather nettled. " I s'pose you thinks I warn't tall enough. Ah! ah! you puts me in mind of the First Liftenant of a frigate I volunteered for, and when I axed him for a captain of a top's vacancy, he eyes me from stem to starn through his quizzing-glass, and says he, 'I thinks,' says he, 'you'd do better for *Billy Ducks*.'* So says I, 'sir,' cocking my hat, and making myself as tall as I could, for I hadn't entered you see,—says I, 'have you got a sailor in your ship as can haul out a reef-earing without going aloft, says I?' 'No,' says he, 'sartainly not.' 'Well then,' says I, 'you aint got a chap aboard as would be at that topsail yard-arm and have the earing out sooner nor better than Dick Summers; so good morning to ye,' said I, making him a low salaam, 'I'll go where I'm better knowed.'— But that's neither here nor there. Let's see, where was I? oh, just going aloft to furl sails.

---

* The naval reader will have no difficulty in understanding this term, but the uninitiated should be told that this title was given to the poultry-man—generally a little man, and still more often, good for nothing else: he ranked with the "loblolly boy," and "midshipman's servant." In the present day things may be different.

"Well, the sail was rolled up smartly—we always beat the foretopmen by half a minute—and the men was passing the gaskets: 'Bear a hand in,' said I; and the midshipman in the top he kept on hailing 'em till a shot stopped him. I was securing the bunt of the sail 'long with my mate; I'd just done, not looking ater the men, and the guns made such a terrible row I couldn't hear 'em; but when I looks along the yard, not a man was left! 'Allo, my lads,' says I, 'you've laid in smartly, but you might have stopped to finish your job though;' but Tom and I laid out, and secured the gaskets, and down we went to our quarters."

"Well, my man,' said the First Leftenant to me, ater the action was over, 'you had a narrow 'scape that time furling the topsail.' 'Why yes, sir,' said I, 'but we gets used to it in time.' 'What,' says he, 'used to losing all your topmen in that way!' 'What way?' says I, 'sir.'

'Why didn't a shot take all your men's heads off?' and it only then come into my mind how 'twas the men had got in so soon. You see a shot had passed along the yard, and took all their heads off, without our knowing anything about it."

Whew! and loud laughter, and clapping of hands resounded from all sides.

" Let him go on," said Fat Jack, as soon as the noise had in some measure subsided; " he aint half done yet."

" Well," continued Slender, " when we hauled aboard the main tack, all the heads rolled down on the booms, for the main-yard men had rolled 'em up in the mainsail. If you don't believe *me* ask old Toby—he was captain of the afterguard."

" Oh yes, it's all true," grunted old Toby; " but I wish you wouldn't kick up such a row." He then sank again into his lethargic state.

" Why I don't see such a deal of wonderment in that after all," said Fat Jack—" maybe you thinks this isn't true what I'm going to tell you, but that you must do as you please about; but when I belonged to the *Oudacious,* one of the

Channel fleet under Lord Howe, we had the battle with the French fleet, you know"——

"What made you cut and run the first day?" asked Peters.

"There was never a ship in the 1st of June that did her duty better than the Oudacious on the 29th of May, and I don't care who says it," answered Fat Jack. "Why if our Captain had kept his wind that day, as a good many of the shy cocks did, we might have been in the 1st of June as well as any on 'em—but no, as soon as there was a chance there was slap at 'em, and no waiting for company. It's the opinion of many 'sides me, that if the other ships had a come down as they ought, and as the Oudacious did, there wouldn't have been anything to do at all on the 1st of June; so none of your jibes, Mr. Tom—we warn't Cæsars, not a bit of it. I was stationed at the fourth gun from forward on the lower deck, and looking aft along the deck, a couple of forty-two pounders from the three-decker close alongside—that's the *Revolutioner* as struck to us afterwards—passed close to me one of each side, and (it's true every word)

I was just Dick Slender's shape at that time, but the wind of the shot squeezed me as flat as a pancake"——

"Or any other *cake*," added Slender, puffing a cloud with infinite satisfaction.

The arrival of 'Frank Johnson' interrupted the laughter occasioned by Fat Jack's story and Slender's wit. This is a very good-natured quiet sort of man, and was invited to partake of the good cheer. But I have not yet described Roberts: and as he makes a good figure in the party, it will be as well to do so now.

Roberts is rather reserved in his manners, and associates little with his wardmates, but when he does his company leaves so favourable an impression on all hands, that his appearance is always attended with great satisfaction. Peters and he are very great friends. Roberts has been a serjeant of marines; he is a tall man near six feet high, with a soldier-like manner and deportment, divested of a great deal of its stiffness.

Silence being restored, Peters requested Roberts would let them hear something about the ghost at Spithead.

"Nonsense," said Roberts, much disconcerted; "you know I have a great dislike to speaking of that, and why do you ask me?"

"Why, to tell you the truth," replied Peters, "I never could get at the rights of the business, although I belonged to the ship, and was Mate of the watch at the time; and as often as I have asked you, you always put me off with some excuse, and promised to tell me another time. I should very much like to hear the story, and I am sure you would not mind letting your old friends here into the secret."

"It is a very long story," said Roberts, "and that is one reason why I never told it to you, and a very sad one also; besides, I fear a mere love and murder story, with a ghost to boot, will not much interest us old men."

"Oh, like the old coachman, we still love to hear the smack of the whip," said Peters; "so pray don't make that an excuse."

"Oh, do let us hear that story," said little Jerry, "because I was always fond of ghosts and such like things. I caught one once after a long battle, and see how I suffered," holding up his hand, which still retained the mark of a bite at the side of it.

"Come, let us hear of that, Jerry," said Roberts, glad of any excuse to delay his story; and Jerry Jones willingly related the story contained in the following chapter.

CHAPTER III.

*The present joys of life we doubly taste,
By looking back with pleasure on the past.*

"Why, when we was fitting out at Plymouth, the old seventy-four—our hulk—was said to be *hanted;* but I soon showed 'em the rights of the business."

"What, I suppose," said Slender, "you frightened him away. If that face of yours wouldn't, I don't know what would."

"You're none so ansome,—so *you* got no room to laugh," replied Jerry, good humouredly.

"If so be as my nose have got a cant, 'taint my faut, but this is how it is: the men in the ship kept losing their blankets out of their hammocks, as they hung up on the orlop, and 'twasn't no good trying to get more, 'cause the

First Leftenant said ve'd sold 'em for to fight a cock wi'.

"Vun night, just after they piped supper, vun of the boys came running up the ladder off the orlop, his teeth chattering, and says he, 'There's the devil down below! I see him come out of the afterhold and run round the deck, and then go down again—he was all black as my hat.' The men said how the boy was a fool, and he couldn't get nobody to listen to him, so he said no more about it. So after supper I played for the dancers, for I was the fidler, till the lights was put out, and down I went to go to bed. I always got a man to hang up my hammock for me, 'cause I couldn't reach to do it myself; and so ven I gets down, I found that somebody else had unlashed it for me, and thinks I that's very good of 'em; but when I got in I found my blanket gone; so, thinks I directly, that's the ghost!

"It vasn't no use kicking up a row about it, so I made the best I could without it, though 'twas very cold. The next night one of my messmates lost his'n, and then we determined to keep a look out. Vell; 'cordingly, when they piped supper, Ned and me, ve goes down below, and stows ourselves away in between the pumps, so that ve thought nobody could see us.

"It was wery dark, for there vas only the sentry's light in the cockpit, and two or three purser's dips forward, vich you all knows don't give much light, and somehow I never liked much being in the dark.

"So ve vaited a little while, and by-and-by ve saw a great tall figure, all black, and he walked along wery slow, and ve thought as ve smelt a strong smell of brimstone; so he went forward, and ve looked after him: but my messmate he wanted to be off: he said he never liked to have nothing to do wi' such things.

"So, says I, I'll go too if you do, and then ve shall never find our blankets; so he agreed to stop a little longer; so the ghost or devil as ve thought him, went along wery slow, and when he got forard, the lights went out! so then ve vas all dark! I begin to feel the water streaming over my nose, and my messmate was shaking terrible——"

"You're sure you didn't knock your knees," said Slender with a grin.

"No, but you would if you had been there," replied Jerry.

"Vell, presently the devil I s'pose spied us out, for he walked aft again as slow as before, and just ven he got abreast the pumps where Ned and me was, he stood stock still, and stretched out his hands just like a play fellow on the stage, and begin to gibber some horrid things, and then groan. But then thinks I, ghosts don't talk, so let's see what you're made of, my pigeon; so I made a bolt right at him, and catching him by surprise, down he vent flat, so I put my knee on his belly, and tried to get hold of him by the throat; but somehow I made a mistake, and shoved my hand into his mouth, and he bit me like a shark!

"I roared out murder! but he keeped on abiting, so then I thought he was indeed the devil. However, thinks I, let's see if he's got any wind in him; so I give him a dig with my knee that made him roar out murder too, and he left go my hand; but you see it was a good smart bite, and I couldn't play the fiddle for a long time afterwards. Vell ven I'd got the upperhand, my messmate he come to help me, and ve secured our prisoner. It turned out that the ghost was a great chap the son of the carpenter of the hulk, as used to make a trade of stealing the blankets; so I got my blanket again, and that was all I cared for."

"Well done, old Jerry—I shouldn't have given you credit for so much," observed Roberts; "and I am sure one ghost story is quite enough for one night, so you had better let me off."

"No, no," shouted all hands.

"There will be plenty of time after tea," said Peters; "and I am sure these old fellows will pass their time better here than in a public-house."

"Well," said Roberts, "if you are determined, I will, to please you, do so; but I promise you it is a long story, and you may think a tedious one. So if you will assemble here after tea, I will endeavour to forage out the written life of the man Peters is thinking of, and read it to you."

Old Toby had, while Jerry was relating his miraculous discovery of a thief, fallen into a sound sleep, every now and then snoring aloud; thereby distracting the attention of Jerry's hearers, and detracting from the applause he considered his due. In return for the interruption thus occasioned, that personage, and Slender, who was always rife for fun, amused themselves with burning corks, and smutting the large and sonorous nose of the sleeping Toby: they marked him for the "king's own," by an inverted broad arrow, and the bright vermillion, which glowed beside the smut, united in producing a very ludicrous and amusing contrast.

"Did you ever hear old Toby," said Peters, —" his being asleep puts me in mind of it—tell the story of his stealing the Commodore's broad pendant at Chatham? He was a nimble boy at that time as ever was seen, but even then rather fond of sleep."

"No," replied they, "how was that?"

"Why, he tells the story much better than I

can. It was when he was a boy in one of the ships laid up at Chatham. His master was the boatswain of her, and there was only the three warrant-officers, with two or three boys, to keep watch on board. The guard-boat from the Commodore's ship was rowing about all night, and if they passed a ship that did not hail them, they would go alongside and endeavour to take anything they could get hold of, and carry it ashore in the morning to the Commissioner's office in the dock-yard.

"One night his master, the boatswain, had the first watch, and having been ashore all day on duty at the dock-yard, he felt very tired, and told the boy (Toby) to keep a look-out, while he went down into the galley to smoke a pipe. He went down and fell fast asleep. The boy, not accustomed to keeping his eyes open, fell asleep also, and the guard boat passing, hailed them; when, receiving no answer, they went alongside, and actually unshipped the bell from its place, and carried it quietly over the side without being found out.

"At twelve o'clock the boatswain awoke from

his sleep, and going to strike the bell, found it gone. He immediately knew who had taken it: he called to Toby, and after bestowing plenty of *blessings* on him, said to him, ' Now, there's only one thing can save my warrant, and if you don't get it for me, I'm done;—I must have the *Commodore's broad pendant* before to-morrow morning.'

"He accordingly got into the punt alongside, and took the boy with him; then pulling softly ahead of the Commodore's ship, dropped under her bows, and Toby got hold of the mooring-chain. From thence he went up by the bobstays, and got to the bowsprit. He then walked slowly up by the forestay into the foretop; and then he got by the maintopmast-stay to the masthead, and finally to the truck, where, unbending the flag, he stuffed it into his bosom. As it was the night pendant it was not very large; so, returning the same way unobserved, he got down again to the mooring-chain, and giving a low whistle, the boatswain, who was some little distance off, dropped under the bows, and took him in.

found my bell gone at twelve o'clock last night, I sent aboard your ship, and got your broad pendant to save my warrant.'

"'My broad pendant!' exclaimed the Commodore, in the greatest consternation—'my broad pendant, did you say?'

"'Yes, your honour; and if you will just step outside I will show it to you flying at the flag-staff of my ship.'

"Accordingly, the Commodore and all his retinue went out, and sure enough there was the pendant as the boatswain had said. The flag had, it seems, been missed in the morning, and put down as blown away. 'Oh,' said the Commodore, 'the boatswain has completely weathered me; I had better say no more about it.'"

"Accordingly," said Slender, chiming in, "the old boatswain *bore off the bell.*"

The supper-bell now warning them of the hour of six, they went in search of their basons and spoons, and away they trudged to the hall, to get their supper and tea in one.

The halls into which they go, are under

the Painted Hall and Chapel; the one containing eight hundred, the other six hundred men; lighted with gas, and furnished with tables and stools. The men are arranged in messes of four each, and their provisions brought them, by pensioners paid for the purpose, in a can, or dish. To the hall which is situated under the Painted Hall, it is now necessary to transport the attention of the reader, and by following close in Toby's wake,—not a very good one, it must be observed,—he may perhaps be repaid his labour.

CHAPTER IV.

"Tut! tut! said the stranger, I have been at the promontary of noses; and have got me one of the goodliest and jolliest, thank Heaven, that ever fell to a single man's lot."
TRISTRAM SHANDY.

TOBY, innocent of the decoration his nose had undergone, awoke by the well known sound of the bell, which had also led to the dispersion of the others; he arose, and mechanically entering his cabin, took his bason, &c. from its customary shelf, shoved his hat firmer over his eyes, and made tolerable progress to the place of refection, unheeding and unheeded.

On his arrival at his table, he found that one of his messmates, who sat opposite, named Peter Felt, a short thick-set fellow, who had evidently finished the contents of his ale bottle, was there before him; but as few civilities were considered necessary, so Toby took no notice of him. Any other person might have seen that it was Peter's full intention to sport with Toby's peculiarity of taste, in regard of his "nose painting;" and that he had made up his mind to insult, if possible, that prominent member of Toby's countenance.

Toby took up the loaf of bread which was to serve for his and his messmate's evening meal, and being cook for the day, he drew his knife from its leathern sheath, and wiping it carefully on the sleeve of his coat, divided the loaf in four equal parts. He then placed the four pieces side by side, on the table, in order that his messmates might each take their choice; himself keeping the portion left. He then pulled off his hat, put it under the stool, and sat down to wait patiently until such time as the grace should be said, and the can of tea brought for their use.

Toby was ever considered a man of few words; and on this occasion he sat without even uttering a grunt, and appeared to be totally oblivious.

Not so Peter: who, encouraged by the other two messmates who had arrived, continued by all the means in his power, short of actual contact, to disturb the reverie of the quiet Toby. He pointed openly to the nose; uttered a thousand sparkling witticisms on its size and weight; and ended by reaching across the table, seizing hold of the nose with both hands, and shaking it as if he would cause dislocation.

Toby at the instant was getting up to pour out the can of tea, which had just been deposited upon the table. His first act, after the rude treatment his nose had received, was to put his hand to that part, to ascertain that it was not entirely gone; his second, to lift the smoking can from the table, which contained full two quarts of hot tea, and pour it, not very gently, over the head of the offending Peter.

Peter roared with anguish. The men at the table, who had long been viewing the proceedings of Toby, and his messmates, in expectation of some such results, now got up from their seats, clapping their hands, and shouting " Bravo, Toby!"—"Go it, Peter!"—"At him again, my hearty!" with many other stimulating gesticulations and expressions.

Peter having recovered the first painful emotions arising from Toby's warm retort, got up from his seat, and planted a severe blow on Toby's optics; but Toby was not to be easily daunted, especially when his blood was stirred by such indignities. He retained his hold of the empty can, and returned Toby's blow with it, making the tin pot rattle against Peter's scull.

Thus did these fierce combatants bandy their fierce looks, and fierce blows. Blood was shed on both sides; for Toby battered the thick head of Peter with his weapon, until the bottom of the vessel separated, leaving a raw edge to work upon; and the purple stream found its way also from Toby's afflicted nose. When, lo! a man in authority approaches, and each sinks down to his place. But they must both be apprehended as violators of the peace, and conveyed prisoners to the main-guard. Thus, for the present the matter must rest.

"A fine scrape you have got poor old Toby

into, Master Jerry," said Roberts to him, as soon as he returned to the ward.

"How so?" asked Jerry.

"Why in smutting his face," replied Roberts; "the poor old fellow has been fighting with one of his messmates, for playing tricks with his nose; and he is now a prisoner at the main-guard."

"Well, I'm wery sorry," said little Jerry; "but to-day is 'valking day*', you know, and vun ought to have a lark now and then; but I dare says he vill be let off easy."

"Why, I am very much afraid it will be a council job," said Roberts; "for old Toby has nearly broken the fellow's head, besides knocking the bottom out of the can."

"Sarved him right!" said Slender Dick—"had no business to touch his nose; and 'twasn't any wonder he burnt his fingers at it; 'tis all the world like a red-hot salamander."

"You had better take care, Master Dick," said Roberts; "for I dare say the question will be asked, 'Who smutted his face?'"

---

* The common name among the men for the festival day.

"Vell," said Jerry, "then ve'll swear he tumbled under the fire-place, wont ve, Dick?"

"Yes, that will do capital well," answered Dick.

Peters and the others—with the exception of Toby, who was in confinement—now entered, and in the course of a little while settled themselves in their places.

The ward is *nominally* lighted by an oil lamp, suspended in the centre of it; but in reality there is—

"No light, but rather darkness visible."

Candles are not allowed; and the serjeant (for as Roberts assumes that character, we will so designate him for the future) was obliged to go to his private store for one; with which, when lighted, he returned to his cabin to search for the manuscript.

While he is so engaged we will take advantage of the light to examine what sort of a place this cabin is. As before mentioned, the cabins are about seven feet square; at the side of this one is the bed place, not quite three feet broad, occupying the whole length of the cabin. Everything here is remarkably neat; the bed has chintz hangings before it, and upon it a clean white counterpane, which is private property. Over the bed's head is a well-executed drawing, in a black frame, of a very interesting young woman, supposed to be a portrait of Roberts's wife; and the bulkhead at the side of the bed is hung with spoils taken from the enemy, such as swords, pistols, &c. The chest containing the manuscript, and his clothes, pulls out from under the bed. Two or three shelves round the cabin are appropriated to books, which appear to have been well selected. In short, there is every comfort a man requires. Here he has " meat, clothes, and fire;" and if Contentment were to be met with in any place, I should think she would probably be found here.

The serjeant having, after searching some time, found the packet he wanted, returned to the party, and seating himself in the large arm-chair, resigned by Peters to him, drew it close to the table; and with a huge serving mallet before him, assumed the office of president. Then carefully cleaning his spectacles with a piece of wash-leather, he adjusted them on his well-adapted nose.

"Before I commence reading this story to you," he said, "I must tell you that I was serjeant of marines, and that the hero of the tale, poor Ned Cummings, belonged to my party. From the first moment I saw him I took the greatest interest in him. He was a tall, handsome young man, about twenty years of age, rather fair, with light hair, and eyes which at times, when he was animated, flashed with lightning; yet withal he was generally so dejected, as to make some of the party, and I for a time among them, think he was mad. He had the heart of a lion when roused, but at other times he was meek as a lamb.

"We had been three years together in different ships before we were separated entirely—in what manner I will relate to you after I have read you his narrative. Three or four months before the catastrophe—(excuse my hard words, Dick) —we were on our homeward voyage, having been stationed for the latter part of our time in the Mediterranean. I was walking the gangway with Cummings—for we were always on the most friendly terms—and expressing my joyful anticipations on returning to my wife and child, who were awaiting with anxiety my coming. To my surprise he did not appear to look forward to our arrival with any satisfaction, but on the contrary with a sort of dread.

"I had never inquired into his affairs, as I disliked being thought prying; but I called to mind that he had never to my knowledge kept up any correspondence with any one at all, unless indeed that he wrote letters for nearly all hands—for he was the best-natured young fellow in the ship; and I remembered also that frequent questions were asked about him by an old comrade of mine, who was a colour-serjeant at Portsmouth, with the request that I would not mention the same to him. When I considered these things, I thought there was something mysterious, and I could not forbear asking him what made him so sorrowful. He turned to me, and said, with an earnestness I cannot forget, 'Roberts, if you knew what a weight I carry here,' pointing to his heart, ' you would not be surprised at my sorrow. Here,' he said, ' is nothing but misery.'

"As I saw he was sad, I said no more. We arrived, and the ship was paid off at Portsmouth. I can answer for my own happiness, and for the time lost sight of Cummings; but we had not been many weeks in barracks, before my party was ordered to re-embark on board the ——— frigate, just commissioned for the East Indies.

"We were then again brought together; but I observed, with much concern, a very great alteration in my poor young friend. Still he was never absent from his duty, but appeared to feel great relief from being employed, as he was, at the dockyard. One night, just before we went out of the harbour, he desired to speak with me. We went on deck, and he said, ' Roberts, you have always been my kind friend, and have for some years made this life endurable, and God will bless you. It is now nearly all over. I don't think I shall ever again leave England.'

"What!" I said, "don't you mean to go out with us?"

"I do not mean to desert," he replied, "nor yet to accept the discharge which has been offered me for that affair in the Mediterranean; and yet," he added after a time, "I shall get it before long."

"You speak in riddles," I said.

"The riddle will soon be explained," he replied. "But here," producing a packet from his bosom—"here is my will for you—the little I possess is yours. You will find there also a letter to my poor old master. I have never seen him but for a moment since an event"——here his feelings overcame him, and he was unable to finish the sentence. After a pause he went on—"You will find there also an account of my short miserable life. You will, after reading it, know that you have fostered a *murderer!* I cannot tell you more now—that will explain all—but let me beg you will not break the seal; and if, as *will not be,* my presentiment is untrue, return it me when we are clear of the Channel; if otherwise, open it, pity my fate, and judge me not harshly."

"I endeavoured to laugh, and then to reason

him out of his gloomy forebodings, in vain; and I abided strictly by his directions. A short time proved the correctness of his anticipations, and I was therefore at liberty to open the packet he had entrusted to me. I found in it the papers I will now read to you. They are a history of his life, and one of the most affecting letters I ever read, for his late master; which, for reasons I will afterwards give, was never delivered."

After snuffing the candle, and clearing his throat with a few short prefatory hems, the serjeant commenced in a clear voice reading the narrative which we shall give in the following chapter.

CHAPTER V.

> "I have unclasped
> To thee the book, ev'n of my secret soul."
> SHAKSPEARE.

"You,[*] my kind friend, to whom I am indebted for such numerous good offices, whose kind counsel, and entertaining company, have made my latter days comparatively happy, ought not to be ignorant of my previous life. I take it as one of the greatest proofs of your sincere friendship, that you have never endeavoured to wring from me that which would have given me inex-

---

[*] The compiler of these stories begs to state, that the authenticity of the MS. which he has here transcribed, rests entirely upon Serjeant Roberts' assertion, and excuses himself from any responsibility for the facts related, which might, without this avowal, rest upon him.

pressible pain to tell you; and indeed, I had determined never to disclose to any one the secrets of my heart. Yet I cannot hide them any longer from you; and should you ever have a son, you can read to him the melancholy life which I am now about to transcribe. Bid him beware! from my example, how he lets his passions overcome his reason! Show him the cause of my misery; my forgetfulness of my God, at a time when, of all others, I ought most to have remembered him; and exhort him, ere a wish for any earthly thing, or a discontented murmur is suffered to escape his lips, to whisper, 'Thy will be done.' Had I done this, how different might have been my lot! But I was a rebel; I rebelled, knowing the extent of my sin; I shut my eyes to the consequences, and rushed in that way to the encounter. It is now too late to retrace my steps: a short time only remains to me; but I thank God I am prepared for the change. My trust and hope is that the God who is omniscient is not unmerciful.

"I was born and educated at P———, a few miles from Portsmouth. My father kept a tavern there, and accumulated some property. My mother died while I was an infant, and my father then married the bar-maid; whose delight was, to do me all the injury in her power. My early life was a constant scene of discord, and my only place of rest was my school. My half brothers and sisters were numerous; but if my brothers were superior to me at home, at school they dared not dispute my powers. I learnt everything which my schoolmaster could teach, with an avidity that surprised and delighted him. Not so at home: my brothers reported my success at school, which had the effect of increasing to a great degree the hatred and jealousy of my step-mother.

"By the time I was thirteen years old I had a tolerable knowledge of Latin; could write a good hand, was a very good arithmetician, and was in short considered by my father, much against my step-mother's wish, fully competent to keep the account-books of the house, and was installed in that office accordingly. It was far from my wish either; for I preferred my school, for the reasons I before stated. I had peace there; but at home there was none for me. I would willingly forget all these things, but they crowd upon my memory. My father alone had affection for me, and he dared not often show it. But I must hastily pass over this part of my life—for I cannot dwell upon so unpleasing a subject—and at once come to the cause of my being sent abroad into the world.

"It happened that a small neighbouring public house, the property of my father, had received a quantity of goods from us, for which payment was to be made by instalments. On one occasion I received an instalment of ten pounds, giving the man an acknowledgment, and putting the money into the till as usual; but, being suddenly called away, I omitted to enter the amount in the proper book. My stepmother, who I knew was much in the habit of robbing the till, to support her extravagance, was near the bar at the time I received the money, and observing that I had not made a note of the sum in the book, she took out the money I had put into the drawer, and I suppose spent it.

"Some little time afterwards the man came for a settlement; he produced the vouchers he had received, and I distinctly remembered the different payments, but still they and the entries did not agree. This was the time for my stepmother. I was of course accused of purloining the ten pounds, discharged from my employment with disgrace, and condemned to wander about the house with my hands in my pockets.

"I was fourteen years of age, when, through the interest of my more than father, my schoolmaster, I was recommended to Mr. S——, a printer of Portsmouth. My father was glad to give his consent to my being bound an apprentice, and with no sorrowful feelings I wished good-bye to all in his house. So great was the rancour of the family against me, generated by the wretch in shape of a woman, their mother, that I retained not a spark of attachment for one of her children; and only on one occasion, the death of my poor father, two years afterwards, did I again visit them. His life, although not one of downright injustice, had been anything but Christian; and what was my horror to hear him on his death-bed own himself an atheist! His last words were dreadful blasphemy! I rushed from the house ere his corpse was cold, and never from that hour returned to it.

"A will was produced after his funeral, giving the whole property to his widow and her children, with the exception of the sum of five pounds, to buy me a suit of mourning, which I was too proud to accept. The unmerited disgrace heaped upon me led to the most happy change in my situation; and I can look back upon five years of almost uninterrupted bliss.

"Extremes of any sort, especially of happiness, are never lasting; and so I have found it. Let that man shudder to whom a long series of undisturbed prosperity has been allotted.

"My excellent master, Mr. S., was a widower, and had an only daughter, about my own age; her name was Clara. It is not surprising that I, whose heart had never before known what it was to feel attachment, should have clung to a being so beautiful, to my warm imagination, as she was. I can only compare her to the creation of a soul-enchanting dream, adorned with every charm which fancy can picture.—As a vision she seemed to me, and as a vision she faded!

"My master had a very good business, and learning the trade occupied for a season all my time and attention. My assiduity soon attracted his favour, and after my daily labour he gave me permission to pass my leisure hours in his little library. I was passionately fond of reading, and did not fail to avail myself of his kindness. Yet I confess that this place had still stronger attractions for me than the books it contained, and often my wandering eyes were more directed to Clara's waving curls than to the page before me. Clara was also fond of reading; but her books and mine were of a very different kind. As I became upon more intimate terms, she often asked me to read to her, and then all books were alike to me. She generally preferred some mushroom of the day, in the shape of a novel; but her wish was a law to me, which I never attempted to dispute.

"How rapidly this my day of happiness passed! the fatigues of the business were lost in anticipation of the hour which was again to restore me the society of Clara. I was soon held in the light of one of the family, and as the period of my apprenticeship drew nigh, was relieved from all the drudgery, and considered by my master worthy of being trusted with the whole weight of the business; which his increased age and infirmities rendered irksome to him.

"Clara was my constant companion. If I were to say I loved her, it would not express a tithe of my affection. I own my sin. She was the idol which I daily worshipped! I had not the smallest desire of pleasing any other being, heavenly, or earthly, but Clara. It signified not to me—the church we constantly frequented, or the places we visited in our occasional rambles—Clara was the only object of my attention. I forgot the Creator entirely, in the presence of the creature!

" My impiety is severely, though not unjustly, punished. My crime is one my heart has since acknowledged; but grievous must my expiation of it be. My heart grew to hers with my growth, and with my strength my attachment strengthened.

"Even now my sinfulness, at times, makes me think that Heaven, without her, would be but an imperfect state. And yet, although at this time I can so clearly define my feelings, I then did not know them. We were rarely separated from each other for a whole day; and I therefore knew not the happiness I enjoyed, until it was torn from me.

"Her father was pleased with my attachment, which he must have seen; and his kindness was such as must ever endear his memory to me. The remembrance of my ingratitude to this most worthy creature, adds greatly to my sorrow! His sickness latterly had confined him almost entirely to the house, and Clara and I sought who should best administer to his comforts.

"It was my delight to read to him, and he, having great taste, contributed largely to my instruction and pleasure; leading me to such works as contained the best information, and the most beauties. His favourite, Milton, was constantly at his side, and he used to say, that although he knew nearly every line of the Paradise Lost by heart, he still derived as much pleasure as ever, from its perusal. He was a good Latin scholar; and by his help I was soon able to read the best Latin authors.

"One evening, after I had been reading to him, he told me it was his intention, if I were willing, to take me into partnership, as soon as my indentures were out; but, at the same time, professed his willingness to assist me in any other view of life I might have formed. I told him I had not an idea separate from his family, and hesitated not to declare to him my passion for Clara. He heard me with signs of satisfaction which I could not mistake; yet plainly told me I should have much to contend with, in his daughter's disposition. The consent he gave me was enough, and I was happy! I soon found an opportunity of telling Clara my hopes were fixed on her; she gave me such assurances as satisfied me; and a lock of her hair was a sufficient pledge.

"One lovely summer's evening, we rambled

over the Southsea Common. The cool, refreshing air had enticed large numbers of people there, but no heart bounded lighter at that time than mine. I had everything in prospect which constituted happiness, nor one fear of the prospect's being an illusion!

"At length we reached the castle, and entering it, mounted to the ramparts to view the fleet at anchor, at Spithead. There were several other visitors, and we paraded round the walls. Happy had it been for me, if that had been the last of my existence! Among the company present was an officer of the Navy, a Lieutenant. The world pronounced him handsome, and he may have been so. I could not help remarking his ardent gazing at Clara, as he passed; which, as we walked to and fro, he did frequently. It did not cause me any uneasiness, as I knew it to be a kind of custom with people of this class; and considering that my Clara's eyes needed not a sentinel, on leaving the place, I banished the circumstance from my mind.

"Clara, by means of some of her female friends, had lately formed an intimacy with a family outside the town, and as her visits were principally in the day-time, I had no opportunity of accompanying her, even if it had been wished; and I had so much confidence in her truth, that I never offered the smallest objection to her going anywhere without me.

"She went one evening to a party at that house, to which, being a stranger, I was not invited; but knowing the time she would be returning, called for her to bring her back. This was a few weeks after the walk just mentioned. I perceived, with sorrow, a great change in her manner, and entreated her to tell me if I had offended her. But, all my powers were unable to restore entirely her usual good-nature. This was the beginning of the tempest, which has overthrown and crushed for ever my structure of happiness! I retired to my bed to think rather than to sleep; thoughts, before the most distant, now crowded round me; the most dismal, yet indistinct, fancies hovered about my mind. At length I slept.

"I dreamt I was walking along some strange road, when, on a sudden, the little packet, containing the lock of hair given me by Clara, which I had constantly worn suspended round my neck, had, by some means, got outside my waistcoat; and before I had time to restore it to its usual place, next my heart, it was snatched from me by a man who, at the instant, rushed past me. He endeavoured to escape from me by running, but I pursued, and overtook him. Methought, as he turned, I remembered his face, and eagerly demanded that of which he had robbed me. He resisted; a scuffle ensued, and we both fell, but he underneath. I hastened to seize the prize, but at the instant a tremendous gust of wind carried it aloft in the air, and bore it from my sight.

"I awoke with the anguish I felt, and searched for my treasure: I found it in its place, and again slept. The same dream returned to me, with the addition, that on looking at my overthrown antagonist, I discovered him to be dead!

"I arose from my bed, and as day had broken, dressed myself, and sought, by a walk in the country, to dispel the gloomy horrors of the night; but all in vain, and I spent the day in ruminating on this strange dream.

"Clara was later than usual to breakfast; and still the cloud remained on her brow, which had caused me the night before such painful forebodings. She went again the next evening to the house of her new friend, telling her father and me, that she should be late before she returned; and that the gentleman of the house would save me the *trouble* of calling for her.

"Her father remonstrated with her on the impropriety of her conduct, but doting as I did, I ventured to make excuses for her, which he unwillingly heard. It was not that I did not feel the slight put upon me, which made me interfere in her behalf; but because I could not endure that Clara should be disappointed.

"I determined, however, for once to be a spy upon her actions, and accordingly, left the house unknown to any one, and loitered about the place where she was; in order that I might see by whom, on her return, she was accompanied. My suspicion was roused; to know the truth was what I sought: I thought I could endure the certainty better than suspense.

"At length the door opened, and the object I sought issued forth, accompanied—I could not be mistaken—by the self-same officer whom we had met at Southsea Castle. There was a field elevated above the road on which they were walking, and I was thus enabled to listen to some part of their conversation.

"I thought her voice, which was once to my ear the sweetest of music, sounded dismal and harsh, as the croak of the raven! I overheard him mention my name: I heard him call me *printer's boy!* I heard her laugh! It was enough! The seal was affixed to my misery. I had now but one object to live for— it was *revenge!* And this one passion took possession of all my senses, and filled up for a time every crevice of my soul!

"I met her the next morning, but, alas! how changed! The smile which so often had played on her ripe lip, was superseded by the curl of disdain; and my heart sickened, though my sternness remained, as I witnessed her altered conduct. Why, at that moment, I did not accuse her, before her father, of her faithlessness, I know not, except that the ally of revenge, Pride, stood in my way, and would not allow me to acknowledge myself an eavesdropper or a spy. If I had done so then, all might have been prevented.

"I went to my duties after breakfast, and tried by employment to alleviate my sorrows; determined to seek an early opportunity of convincing Clara I was aware of her perfidy. Alas! there is nothing like the present moment. While love, revenge, and pride, were debating within me my proper course of proceeding, Clara was flying from me for ever!

"She left the house without my knowledge, telling her father she was going for a short walk, and I saw her no more! We waited dinner for some time, and still she came not. Her father looked at me as if to read in me the cause; but he could only discover my misery. He took *that* for a knowledge of what he thought,—probably thinking that some trifling quarrel had occurred; and he avoided questioning me. Our untasted dinner was sent away, and still I observed a sullen silence. The evening came—still no Clara. The old man could no longer stifle his feelings.

"'For God's sake, Harry,' said he, 'what is the matter? Where is Clara?' 'Sir,' I replied, with as much firmness as I could muster; 'her absence is as much a mystery to me, as it appears to be to you.' 'Have you quarrelled with her?' he asked. 'No,' I answered, and my grief prevented my saying more. 'For Heaven's sake, leave me not in ignorance; let me know what has become of my child. I will go instantly in search of her.' His vehemence aroused me. 'And I will go too,' said I, brushing away the tears which had found means to disgrace my cheeks.

"Ill as the poor old man had previously been, he appeared in an instant to have thrown off his infirmities. We sallied forth, and walked at a rapid pace, almost involuntarily, to the house to which she had gone the night before. The lady stated, in answer to his inquiries, that

Clara had been there in the morning, where she had met Lieutenant ——, a gentleman intimate with her husband, and that she believed it was her intention, on leaving, to go in a carriage with him to Titchfield, returning the same evening.'

"'And pray,' said Mr. S., after hearing the lady impatiently to an end, 'what part, madam, may *you* have acted in this business?' With some confusion, she replied that frequent meetings had taken place at her house, and that Lieutenant —— was a man of good family and property; and had told her his intentions were most honourable towards Miss S., and that he either would communicate, or had communicated them (she did not remember which) to her father.

"Nothing but the old man's distress exceeded his passion, and he quitted the house, leaving an angry message for his daughter on her return, and muttering curses 'not loud, but deep,' on the baseness of this woman's conduct.

"I still refused to mention what I had myself witnessed the night before, and we returned disconsolately to our home. Fully expecting their return, we waited till twelve o'clock, in an agony of mind not to be described; we then retired to rest. I threw myself on my bed in a state of insanity, while the events of the few past days floated in confusion around me.

"The sun at length restored me to a glimpse of reason, and I got up, washed and dressed myself with great care, in my best clothes, in the full determination of pursuing my revenge to the uttermost.

"Early in the morning a letter was brought to the house by a countryman, addressed to my master, who told a long round-about story as to the manner in which it had come into his possession.

"I took the letter from the man, and questioning him closely, got him to confess that he received the letter from a gentleman at Purbrook.

"I carried the letter to Mr. S——, who hastily broke the seal, and scanning the contents, sank back on his bed in dreadful convulsions. I rang the bell, and sent in haste for a doctor, who lost no time in attending. The convulsions ceasing, he lay for some time in a state of torpor, which the doctor told me was not dangerous.

"I took the letter from him and read it; it was written hurriedly, and evidently dictated by the monster to whom Clara had consigned herself. It stated 'that she was going away to be married to a gentleman of rank and fortune, who was obliged to act in this summary way, as his ship was soon going to sea; but that she hoped in a short time to throw herself at his (her father's) feet, and implore his pardon for the step she had taken.'

I folded the letter up and placed it on the table; I kissed my master's cold forehead, and bade a hasty adieu to the walls which once held all that I loved. All my master's kindness to me, and the acuteness of his sufferings, were forgotten. I had no room in my breast for any other feeling but that of REVENGE; and I *was* revenged!

"At this period what a comfort it would have been had I thought upon my God; yet it was at this moment that I forgot him entirely. I did not try to say 'Thy will be done,' but rushed madly forward, trusting to my own powers, and seeking unaided that which belongs only to God. All my after misery hinged upon this; and thus will it ever be to him that follows my example.

"I knew in an instant, on reading the letter, the fate awaiting poor Clara. But judge her not harshly. Young and artless, she had not known a mother's care, and her beauty proved her bane. Her guards were slender, and such as an imperfect education had raised; while he, the seducer, armed with his master's, the devil's, weapons, easily beat them down. Whatever was the extent of her crime, her punishment exceeded it; and women's crimes rarely go unpunished."

CHAPTER VI.

"I'm invited to Sir John Loverule's butler, and am to be princely drunk with punch, at the hall place; we shall have a bowl large enough to swim in."—Devil to Pay.

"SNUFF the candle, Jerry," said the serjeant; which Jerry proceeded to do, but whether from the obliquity of his vision, or the knock which Slender gave his elbow, I do not know,—he snuffed it out.

"And now," continued the serjeant, glad of the excuse, as soon as the candle was relighted, "as my poor old eyes are nearly tired, I wish one of you would help out the evening with one of your own stories, and I will keep the remainder of this for another night—that is, if you like it, and do not find it too tedious."

"He carries too many guns for me," said

Slender, "I can't stand his two deckers; give me your plain English."

"It is a very touching story, I think," said Frank Johnson, "and it brings to my mind some of my early misfortunes. Ah," continued the old man, with a sort of a sigh, not unlike an asthmatic cough, "I should never have gone to sea but for something in that way."

"Then let us hear it, Frank, by all means," said the serjeant.

"And mind and cut it short," added Slender: "you see there is Old Tim fast asleep already, and Fat Jack's head going like a Chinese mandarin's in a grocer's shop; and I begin to feel a little matter drowsy myself."

Thus instructed, Frank Johnson commenced his story, in nearly the following words:—

"I was born in the parish of St. Pancras, and was never out of the smoke of London until I was eighteen years old. I was 'prenticed to a hair-dresser in Gosling-street; and if I had continued till this time to curl wigs and cut hair, I might have been a man of large property. But somehow, just as I was seventeen years of age,

Betty Saunders fell in love with me, and I couldn't do no less than fall in love with her in return; but, for all that, she told me, she loved nobody, only me. I had not been away more than six or eight months before she married my rival, a footman, saying, as an excuse, that she thought I should never come back again.

"When first I saw the dear creature, she opened the door of her master's house to me—I had to go there every morning, which gave me many an opportunity of getting from her a sweet word or a kind look, and she used to smile so good-natured. She was housemaid.

"One evening I was in the shop, and who should pop in but Betty Saunders. You can't think how my heart did flutter. So she says to me, says she, 'I wants my hair dressed.' 'Certainly, Miss,' said I, 'walk into the back parlour.' So she went in; and when she pulled off her bonnet and cap, her beautiful long red hair —it was rather too red to be sure—fell so fine over her handsome broad shoulders, that I felt in a minute all of a tremble.

"So says I, 'Miss, pray how would you like

it dressed—in the new French curls, or?——
'In the *newest* fashion, certainly, Sir,' says she. So I began, and trimmed, and pomatumed, and made the pinchers hot to curl it; but I could hardly get out a word, my mouth was for all the world like a shut rat-trap; but at last I managed to say, 'Going to the ball at the Red Lion, I suppose, Miss?' 'No, Sir,' said she, 'indeed I keeps no such low company!' and she gave her head a great toss, which unfortunately brought the hot curling irons close to her beautiful fair forehead.

"With that she jumped up in a terrible passion, and gave me such a terrible slap on the cheek that it was burning for a week afterwards. I was so sorry to think I had hurt her, that I did not mind the blow; so I begged her pardon on my knees, and she soon forgave me—she was always very forgiving. I finished her hair in such a style, that when she looked in the glass she quite forgot the burn, and I the box on the ear; and then she wanted to pay me, but I told her I could not think of taking the money, and should be always proud to dress her hair, whenever she wanted it done. So she put the money back into her pocket, and gave me instead such a sweet smile.

"After a time we got very thick, and we began to talk of being married as soon as I was out of my time; but there, you see, it was not to be.

"She invited me one night to a party, which she told me the cook was going to give to her friends, for that her mistress was going to a ball, and her master was away in the country. So about ten o'clock I got leave from my master, as I expected to be out late; and I put on my new bottle-green long-tailed coat, and my best frilled shirt, and cut no bad figure.

"Sure enough there was a capital turn out, and you would have thought, to look at the women, they had been all duchesses. Betty looked so handsome. She was dressed in a beautiful red silk dress that belonged to her mistress, and a pair of white satin shoes. There was about half-a-dozen young men besides me, servants in the neighbourhood, and a great many young women, and there was a fiddler, and plenty to eat and drink.

"So we danced till about twelve o'clock, and I was dancing then with Betty, and was so very happy, when we heard a terrible loud rap at the door. 'Oh dear, there's master at the door!' said Betty—'I know his knock—what *shall* we do?' You never saw such a scampering in all your days. Who is to go to the door?

"Another knock and a tremendous ring at the bell still remained unanswered, and at last the door was broke open, and down rushed the master, with two or three watchmen, into the kitchen. Nearly all the livery servants being better up to such rows, made their escape at the kitchen window, but I and another young chap got catched.

"I might have got away too, but I could not find it in my heart to leave poor Betty in so much trouble; but by the direction of the gentleman the watchmen took charge of me and the other, and carried us away toward the watch-house.

"As chance would have it, we had not gone far when a pressgang surrounded us, and the officer said to the watchmen, says he, ' These are the very fellows we have been looking after, and you must let us have them.'

"The watchmen was taken on an 'unplush,' and as the pressgang seized upon their rattles, they could not make any noise; besides, the officer threatened if they did he would carry them off as well; so I and the other poor fellow were forced along at a quick pace, and carried on board a tender lying off the Tower.

"I told the officer I was 'prentice; and he said, 'So much the better—you are just the sort of chap we want;' and finding it was no use grumbling, I said no more. At last we reached the tender, and they stowed us away down below in such a filthy place, along with all the scrapings of the gaols, and thieves, and vagabonds of all sorts. I thought they would have paid a little more respect to my *bottle-green long-tailed coat.*"

"The next morning at daylight the vessel got under way, and went down the river to her ship, the old Sandwich, the guard-ship at the Nore; but we did not reach there until the next day, when, at about eleven o'clock in the forenoon, we got alongside; and the pressed men were handed up, and sent aft to be mustered.

"For all my troubles, I could not help being pleased with the fine ship I was on board of, and I looked with wonder at everything around me. The largest ship I had ever seen before was a merchant ship, and I thought nothing could be larger. What surprised me most was the immense size of the masts, and then the great ropes which supported them, and I couldn't think how they got there. But they didn't give me much time to think.

"My name was called over, and, after inquiring my age, trade, place of birth, &c., I was ordered to go below to the Doctor, to be overhauled. I kept on telling the people I was a 'prentice, but everybody turned a deaf ear to what I said; so I went down ladder after ladder, with the other men, and thought I was going into the other world. At last I got into a dark place—the cockpit—and was waiting at the bottom of the ladder for my turn to go into the cabin, when all on a sudden I felt myself pulled backwards on the ladder; but I soon got loose again, and, putting my hands behind me, found my coat tails clean gone, entirely! the coat that cost me near three pound, and nearly new! I saw a lot of fellows grinning like a parcel of monkeys behind the ladder, and I swore I would complain of them as soon as I got on deck; and so I did.

"I went up to the First Leftenant, and when I told him my story, he put on a face as grave as a judge; and, says he,—' My lad, there is a set of fellows about this ship that will steal your teeth while you are asleep if you don't keep your mouth shut, and I advise you to be very careful; but,' says he, 'if you can only point out the man that cut off your tails, he shall be severely punished for it.' But, as I could not do that, I was obliged to put up with the loss.

"The men served me all manner of tricks, such as turning my hammock inside-out, and sending me on fools' errands; one sent me to the purser's steward to get my mouth measured for a spoon; until at last I was broke in. I took it all good-naturedly, and they soon left me alone: but there was one fellow, much taller and older than me, who, one morning, washing decks, thought proper to heave a bucket of water over me, for which I knocked him down; and, as we could not fight on deck, we had a turn-to below, directly after breakfast.

"This fellow thought I knew as little about using my fists, as I did an oar, and therefore made sure of an easy victory. We got forward in the eyes of her, and I had my second, and the other man his, and we stripped. I was not at all afraid of him, for I had studied boxing with one of my companions, and in five rounds I turned up my antagonist with as fine a pair of black eyes as he could desire. I got great praise for this; as Dick Jones, for that was his name, had carried it all his own way for a long time.

"I had not been aboard the Sandwich more than a fortnight, when I was drafted into the Venus, Jonathan Faulknor, cruising in the

Channel. Being a smart active young fellow at that time, they did not long keep me as a waister, but stationed me in the fore-top; and I soon became as happy and nimble as any of them.

"I wrote several letters to my master and Betty. My master told me he had applied to the Admiralty Office for my release, but had not got any answer; and Betty told me that some of the silver spoons had been missed from the house the night I was there, and that I was accused of the theft; but she said she did not believe it was me who stole them. She said her master had forgiven her, but turned the cook away: so I thought, all things considered, I had better remain where I was.

"I had been in the frigate about five or six months, and liked the business nearly as well as trimming hair; for we were making a few prizes, and I began to think I might make a fortune at it. But at that time I had never seen the way the prize-money was paid—there's not much as sticks in the splinter netting.*

---

* It was a common saying among the men, as my nautical

"We cruised some time in company with the Nymph, and fought the first action in that war; and though we couldn't manage to secure our prize, yet we did more than any one could expect. Perhaps, if the rights was known, we deserved as much, or more credit than the Nymph; and our Captain deserved as much to be knighted as Captain Pellew did. There was never a better man stepped aboard a ship than Captain Jonathan Faulknor—nor a braver one."

"Wasn't there some law business between your Captains?" asked the Sergeant, interrupting him. "I think I remember some dispute."

"Yes, there was," replied Johnson, "and I'll tell you how it come about. Our Captains thought that, as we cruised in company, it would be as well to enter into agreement to share prize-money alike, whichever ship took the prize; and the ships' companies accordingly

---

readers may know, that the clerk who paid the prize-money went into the main-top and hove the money down on the splinter netting, when all that went through was for the officers, and the rest for the men.

agreed to it; but a day or two after we had fought the action with the Semillante, the Nymph joined us, and ordered us into port. So Captain Pellew thought that, as we had got our whack, the agreement was at an end, and when he took the Cleopatra, wouldn't let us share for her—that's how it was."

"I never knew any good come of those agreements yet," said Roberts; "there's always sure to be some quarrel or other come out of them. But come, let us hear about your action with the Semillante."

"The latter end of the month of May, ninety-three," continued Frank, "nearly three in the morning, at daybreak, a strange sail was reported on the weather-beam. (The Nymph had parted company from us, in chase, a day or two before). She was soon made out to be a large French frigate. She bore up, and ran down to have a look at us, and seeing as tight a little frigate as ever swam in salt water, she hauled to the wind again, and hoisted English colours; but we knew what she was well enough. Well, we made all sail in chace, and cleared for action, determined to let them see what kind of stuff we was made of.

"She let us come up with her, though she was able to sail round us for that matter, and at a little before four o'clock, of a fine summer's morning, we commenced a running fight with her; she still keeping the weather-gage. She kept just about a point before our beam, and being able to choose her distance, had a great advantage over us, because, you see, her guns were eighteens,* and ours only twelves; and our short carronade would hardly reach her, while every shot of hers told.

"But as the wind fell light, she broke off, and we got a little nearer; and, after fighting her for two hours and forty-five minutes, she hauled down her colours,† and expected us to take possession of her, and accordingly we ceased

---

* This is disputed: with what justice, the author does not know—it is said they were twelves.

† This all our Naval historians have entirely omitted, but there are two men, eye-witnesses, one of whom positively asserts it, and, the other says, they were shot away, and not rehoisted until she bore up to rejoin her consorts.

firing; but we had not a boat that would swim, and our masts so much cut that we expected them to fall every minute; and she, seeing us as bad off as herself, made sail across our bows and rehoisted her colours.

"'Put the helm up,' said the Captain, 'and give her another broadside;' which we did, without getting a shot in return, but seeing two strange sail to leeward, our Captain thought we had better refit our rigging, and fish our masts, to get ready for a new customer.

"We afterwards heard that our prize got into port with a good deal of difficulty, and not without the assistance of the crew of an English letter-of-marque she had on board, who was promised their liberty if they lent a hand to save the ship, for she had five-feet water in her hold.

"As soon as the action was over, Captain Faulknor called all hands aft, and said to us—'My fine fellows,' said he, ' you have all done your duty like true British tars, for you have made a large forty-gun French frigate surrender to you, and I only wish I was in a condition to chase her; but,' said he, 'it seems here's something else for you to do; there are two strange sail astern, and I suppose them to be the companions of the ship we have just beat, and I hope, my lads,' says he, 'you won't give the ship away, but stick to her as long as she will swim.'

"With that we gave him three hearty cheers, and then turned to with a good will; got the lower-yards down, fished the lower masts, knotted all the rigging, rove new running-gear, and bent new sails; and by night was all as fresh as ever, and clear of our enemies. Fortunately it was nearly calm all day, or our masts must have gone."

"How many men did you lose?" asked Peters.

"Why," replied Frank, "we had not quite two hundred men aboard when we commenced the action—no marines at all—and out of them we lost about thirty-five killed and wounded; while the French frigate lost more than double that number. Ours was one of your small twelve-pounder frigates, and we had only *thirty-*

four guns in all aboard, two of them twenty-four-pounder carronades, and good for nothing. The Semillante was nearly as big again, had more than three hundred men, and carried forty guns. So that I say our Captain deserved as much praise as Captain Pellew: but just because we didn't bring our prize into port, all our reward was lost."

"That's just the way," said Peters; "John Bull always liked to have something to look at, and then he made sure it must be a great victory. One prize at Spithead gave him more satisfaction than to know that half-a-dozen were at the bottom of the sea. There was many an officer during the last war, who, notwithstanding he did the most gallant actions, yet, for want of being *lucky,* all his good deeds were forgotten."

"But come," said he to Johnson, "let us think of something else: did you ever see Betty any more?"

"Oh, yes," replied Johnson; "I saw her some years afterwards, and found she was a wife, as I told you before, to one of my companions at the ball."

"Ah, them women are a deceitful set," said little Dick,—"what do you say, my hearty, eh?" addressing himself to his neighbour Jerry, and accompanying his question with a slap on his elevated shoulder, which had the effect of rousing him from his *doze*—"A'nt they a bad lot, Jerry?"

"Oh yes," said Jerry, after looking carefully over each shoulder, to be sure his wife was not behind him; "but," he added, "if it vasn't for my vife I should think them all angels."

"Come, let us hear you sing that old song of yours, Johnson," said the Serjeant, "for I don't like to hear the women abused; and what do you know of them after all?"

"I knows 'em well enough," replied little Dick, raising his head with an air af importance: "wasn't I flogged twice all on their account? and didn't I run twice from the Sarvice for them? and I thinks I ought to know a little about them—a woman's a woman all the world over. I tell you what—a woman's just for all the world like the moon—one day she looks full and kindly at you, and then she turns away her head again, when she thinks you like her; and then she turns her back on you altogether. Just when you've got your pockets full of money she will look as bright and good natured as can be; but no sooner is the locker empty than there's good bye to you; you may be off to sea for more, as soon as you like, and the sooner the better. But I should like to hear Frank's song, for all that; so if you will call for order, Mr. President, I dare say he will strike up."

A few thumps on the table with the serving-mallet caused silence, and after a little pressing, Frank Johnson sang the following little ditty, in a pleasing, though rather sentimental, style:—

SONG.

Young Nanny and I were just married,
   Two happier never were seen;
Some said I had better have tarried,
   A bachelor still to have been.
Dear Nanny and I we said—No,—
   We thought their wise sayings all stuff;
For 'tis little we want here below,
   And to gain that our strength is enough.

Enough!—Can that mortal repine,
   Who is blest with the girl that he loves?

Not for kingdoms I'd Nanny resign,
  For her smile my exertions approves;
And, when weary, I reach my cot door,
  Her cherry lips welcome me in,
Nor I know that the world calls me poor,
  Nor care for their riches a pin.

We can sing, we can dance, we can laugh;
  We can love, yes, dear Nanny for ever;
Though not wine, yet the ale-cup, we quaff,
  And grumble we will not—No never!
And why should our hearts wish for more,
  Or value the foolish world's frown?
We have health, and good humour, in store,
  And virtue these blessings to crown.

"Well sang, my old warbler! that's a very capital song," rejoined Dick, after the applause had in some measure subsided. "But, perhaps, after the poor man had been married a little while longer,"——

"Silence, silence!" said the Serjeant; "don't let us hear any more of your scandal about the women—for I dare say you like them as well as any body, after all."

"To be sure I do," replied Dick, "only I can't help seeing what a mischievous set they are for all that; and for that matter I think I know a song that's just my way of thinking: it's as old as myself, but true enough, as all the world knows."

"Shall Jerry accompany you with the fiddle?" inquired Peters.

"No, thankee," replied Dick, "I can't endure Jerry's music; it reminds me of nothing but *grinding scrapers*. I think I can do better without him, if it's all the same. So here goes:" —And he managed to get through the following curious old song:—

SLENDER DICK'S SONG.

St. Patrick was told that the Devil, adrift,
  Was cruising about in the town,
And he thought he could find him and give him a lift,
  And quickly again kick him down.
  And quickly again kick him down.

But how for to catch him the Saint could'nt think,
  His friends were so numerous grown;
And they'd hide him away in some snug little chink,
  Though none his acquaintance would own.
      Though none, &c.

He hunted all round, and he went to each house,
  He look'd under the lawyer's table;
If the Devil had been but as big as a mouse,
  To escape him he had not been able.
      To escape him, &c.

There was none could direct him, though each one had felt
    A rub from his highness profound;
And the Saint had the burning of brimstone smelt,
    So at last the arch-demon he found.
            So at last, &c.

He found him, 'tis true, but in vain all his might—
    The Devil he could'nt turn out;
And like many Saints since he was vanquished in fight,
    And entirely put to the rout.
            And entirely, &c.

If you look, on the morn of a bright summer's day,
    In the arch little Judy's black eye,
There, snug in a corner, you'll see him at play,
    Shooting darts at each passer by.
            Shooting darts, &c.

"Well done, old Dick," resounded from all sides, and even Tim Stuart was aroused by their laughter and applause. "But where did you pick up that?" said Roberts.

"I have known it many years," replied Dick, "and I wonder I remembers it so well; but it serves me to hum over to myself when I am walking about, and I never meet a pretty girl with black eyes, but I always fancy I see the old chap in the corners of them; and then I says to myself—"Ah! there you are again, old boy."

"Let us have another song before we break

up," said the Serjeant, " for I hear the bell ringing, and it will soon be time to turn in. We will just finish this bottle (the reader will believe it required but a small effort to do that), and then say good night."

Peters gave them the old well-known song, " How happy could I be with either;" and, with another from Tim Stuart, the party separated, and retired in good order to their several warm and comfortable bed-cabins.

CHAPTER VII.

> "No! said he, looking up,—I am not such a debtor to the world—slandered and disappointed as I have been—as to give it that conviction.—No! said he, my nose shall never be touched whilst heaven gives me strength.——
> *Tristram Shandy.*

The council room, having been described at full length in the preceding part of this volume, it remains only to state that, into this chamber Toby is about to be summoned, to take his trial for the misdemeanor committed in the dining-hall on the previous evening. In the centre of this room is a large table, or "board of green cloth," at the upper end of which, seated in a capacious mahogany arm-chair, of most extensive powers, is the venerable functionary who hears and disposes of offences against the laws of the Hospital; referring those of greater magnitude to the Council, who sit once a-week.

Offences of a trivial description, committed on festival day, as I before observed, are always overlooked, or lightly visited; while those of a more heinous nature must receive their due punishment, the same as if committed on any other day.

"What complaints have you this morning, John?" asked the Captain, addressing a fine old fellow, the yeoman of the guard, who was, as usual, in attendance.

"There's only one of much consequence, your honour," replied John; "but there was all hands drunk yesterday. Here is the complaint sheet, sir"—handing, among others, a piece of paper, which for the reader's satisfaction I will transcribe:—

"Tobias Williams, for throwing a can of tea over his messmate, Peter Felt; also fighting in the hall at tea-time, last night; also breaking the can and creating a disturbance.

"Witness   " Bo. T. JOHN, regulator.
             " Bo. JOHN SWAYAWAY.
             " MT. WILLM. JACKSON.
             " JAS. ROBERTS.

"Nov. 5, 18—."

"Well, send them in," said the Captain, after reading the above charge; and old John proceeded to execute his orders. "I declare," ejaculated the Captain, "this ale is much too strong for the men! Never an ale-day passes over without some accident,—a broken head, or a broken leg," (query, a timber one,) "or some such mischance."

During this short soliloquy the prisoner and witnesses, who had been waiting outside, were brought in and ranged in order near the table.

Poor old Toby's nose was now—alas! how fallen. It had the sickly hue of a white raspberry; and altogether he looked like a man resigned to the worst. He seemed perfectly aware of his misfortunes, being evidently desirous of eluding observation, and he therefore allowed his late combatant, Peter Felt, to plant himself in front; thus giving that person an opportunity of creating, by his rueful countenance, an interest in the mind of his judge.

Peter seemed to have suffered materially, if one might be guided by the extensive quantity of white plaster upon his face; for just from above his left eyebrow, to his right temple, was a band near two inches in breadth, and a narrower strip extended from half-way down his nose, to where it intersected the broader band.

"Now, John," said the Captain, "will you tell me what you know of this business? It appears a very serious matter."

"Last night at tea, your honour," said the old man, "just after I said the grace, I heard a disturbance, and went to see what it was about, and there I saw this here man, Toby, as they calls him, and this man here a-fighting. Toby had the can in his hand, and was whacking the other over his head, while all the people in the hall was standing up, and laughing and shouting,—'Go it, Toby'—'Give it to him'—'That's the time-of-day.' This is the can, your honour, that I took from him," exhibiting the identical weapon, with the bottom half out.

"Upon my word, you are a dangerous character, Mr. Williams," said the Captain. "Where are you, Sir? Come forward and let me see you:"—a command Toby unwillingly obeyed. "Well, and what did you do with them?" continued the Captain.

"Sent them to the main-guard, your honour, and Peter Felt was obliged to be sent to the doctor to get his head plastered."

"Well, and did the doctor report him much injured?" inquired the Captain.

"Only a little of the bark knocked off," answered John; "the doctor said his *ineffectals* was not hurt."

"His what?" asked the Captain with much surprise.

"His *ineffectals* or *intellectals*, or sumat in that way—I don't mind the words exactly," replied the single-minded being.

"Very well, that will do," said the Captain smiling. "Now, Boatswain John Swayaway," after having with some difficulty deciphered this name. "Let me hear what you know of this affair."

"Your honour," said Swayaway, coming forward with sundry awkward bows and scrapes, "I was boatswain of the main-guard last night, and at twenty minutes past six P.M. these 'ere two men was placed under my charge; and I sent this 'ere man, Peter Felt, to the infirmary to get his head sewed up, for it was bleeding."

"Were the men drunk?" asked the Captain.

"Why, your honour," replied Swayaway, with hesitation, "I can't say as how they was drunk, your honour, 'twoudn't be right of me."

"Then were they sober, sir?" said the Captain with some haste.

"Why, no, your honour, not 'zactly sober," retorted the boatswain, giving his head a doubtful scratch.

"Answer me this question, sir," said the Captain with vehemence. "Were they drunk, or were they sober?"

"Why, your honour," said the boatswain, not able any longer to evade, "if I must say it, I thinks they was a little matter intosticated in liquor."

"If you must say it, sir!" repeated the Captain, "to be sure you *must say* it, sir. It is strange you men can't answer a plain question without so much trouble. Let me see—who is the next witness?—William Jackson, mate. Well, sir, and what do you know about this fight?"

"I'm one of the mess, your honour," replied Jackson, advancing nimbly.

"Well, and how did the row begin, and what hand had you in it?"

"Me, your honour!" said Jackson, surprised, "I had nothing to do with it, sir!"

"Then, sir, you neglected your duty; you ought to have had something to do with it," answered the Captain. "You a mate, and suffer this disturbance! you deserve to be put on the complaint yourself. How long have you been a mate, sir?"

"Six weeks, your honour," replied the downcast Jackson.

"Then, sir, mind this never happens again. Go on with your evidence, sir."

"Why, sir—your honour," said Jackson, "we got talking of old times, your honour, and laughing about one thing and t'other, and by and by that man," pointing at Toby, "comes to his place, and his face was rather smutty, your honour. So he thought as how we laughed at him, and then he called us all manner of names; he called me a *Michiman's** *warmint*, your

---

* Query—did Jackson ever serve in the capacity of Midshipman's Steward?

honour, and he called Peter there, as got his head cut, an old *Brummagem smasher*, your honour; and abused all hands, without our saying a word to him, but 'cause he was quite drunk, your honour—"

"That's a lie," grunted Toby, interrupting him.

"Silence, sir," said the Captain in a loud tone. "We'll hear you presently."

"And then," continued Jackson, "when Peter said sumat about his nose, he tuck hold of the can jist as the bluefrockman put it on the table, and hove it slap over him, and it all went down his poll, and 'twas very hot, your honour. And then they fought over the table, and Toby beat his head all to a mummy, and all we could do wouldn't stop him, your honour, until the regulator come and parted 'em. He's a very *refectory* man in the mess *al*-ways; and that's all I knows about it, your honour." So saying, he made a bow and retired.

"Well, Master Williams, or Toby, or whatever they call you," said the Captain, addressing our crest-fallen friend, who had again taken up a backward position, "these are very fine doings—very fine doings, indeed, sir! You might have killed the man, sir, and then what would have been the consequence?" But Toby said not a word, nor moved a muscle. "Are there any more witnesses? Oh, here's another, I see,—James Roberts."

"Your honour," answered our old friend the serjeant, coming forward, who, for Toby's sake, had got himself put down as a witness.

"Well," said the Captain, "I am rejoiced that you saw the transaction, Roberts, because I am sure you will tell me the plain truth."

Accordingly Roberts recounted in a straightforward manner the facts; how that the provocation had been entirely on the other side, and that until Peter Felt had pulled his (Toby's) nose, he (Toby) had conducted himself in an orderly and peaceable manner, nor shown the smallest disposition to pugnacity; at once placing the affair in a very different light, and turning the table upon the hitherto triumphant party.

"And so, sir," said the Captain, addressing

himself to Peter Felt, when he had heard Roberts patiently to an end—" you pulled the man's nose, did you, sir?"

"I only went to brush the smut off, your honour," replied Felt, dismayed by the evidence given by Roberts, and his natural skin fast approaching in colour to the artificial part.

" He almost unshipped it," grunted Toby in an under tone.

" Hold your tongue, sir.—Oh! you only went to brush the smut off, sir!" addressing Peter. " And pray, sir, what right had *you* to touch another man's nose, even if it was to brush the smut off? And," continued the Captain, " I think, sir, you richly deserved all you got. What! pull a man's nose, indeed! You were served perfectly right—be off about your business; and mind, Williams, never go into the hall again with a smutty nose."

" No, your honour; thankee," answered old Toby, as he made his best bow and speediest exit, much delighted and surprised with his favourable dismissal.

We will now return to the —— ward, and

consider the evening to be again returned, and the same party to which I last night introduced you, re-assembled; and that old Toby, whose nose is again glowing as brightly as ever, has resumed his winter's station in the corner.

It will, perhaps, be worth while to account for the occupants of the remaining cabins; let us, therefore, try back a little. We know of the boatswain, Harry Swallow, who has nominal charge of the ward, but who is generally only present when absent—*i. e.* drunk. The next in order is our little friend, Jerry, mate of the ward; then comes Tom Peters, three; Jim Roberts, alias the serjeant, four; Tim Stuart, five; fat Jack, six; little Dick Slender, seven; Frank Johnson, eight; and old Toby, nine.

Now there are, as I said before, fifteen cabins, out of these I have accounted for nine: there are three married men who sleep out, who only look in now and then; one nurse's cabin, and at present two vacancies, which may soon be filled up. The executives you know.

The table is now shorn of its ornaments; no rum-bottle or pannikin is to be seen thereon, and the serving mallet to keep order is now rendered useless; but the serjeant is seated at the table, and ready to recommence the perusal of the manuscript. Yet before he begins, he is desirous of gathering the suffrages of his audience, as to whether they are interested therewith.

Peters expressed a great wish to hear it, knowing the consummation; and the others, expecting something wonderful, joined in requesting the serjeant to proceed.

He complied with their wishes, as will be seen in the following chapter.

CHAPTER VIII.

> " Had it pleased Heaven
> To try me with affliction ; had he rained
> All kinds of sores, and shames, on my bare head ;
> Steeped me in poverty to the very lips ;
> Given to captivity me, and my utmost hopes ;
> I should have found in some part of my soul
> A drop of patience :—
> But there, where I have garnered up my heart ;
> Where, either I must live, or bear no life ;
> The fountain from the which my current runs,
> Or else dries up ; to be discarded thence !—
> *Othello.*

"I MADE up my mind to proceed instantly in quest of the fugitives, to revenge myself on the seducer—for such I considered him to be—of Clara. I had but a guinea belonging to me. I determined not to take money from my master, nor would I borrow from the men ; so hastily tying up an extra shirt, and taking a stout cudgel for my companion, I started at about ten o'clock in the morning, on my wild pursuit.

"It was the latter end of July. I remember it was the first day of Portsdown fair. I had not money enough to take coach; besides, I knew not in what direction to go, and I therefore came to the resolution of seeking information of them on foot at Purbrook. I walked at a rapid pace through the town, cautiously avoiding all with whom I was acquainted; for this purpose also, I left the main-road for another track across the fields; and I passed on unmolested by any of the gay parties flocking to the fair.

"What a wilderness was the world become to me! How did my heart sicken, as I approached the well-known stile, which once had formed the boundary of my rambles, with the all-engrossing and then virtuous Clara! It was there I had carved our initials; it was there I had vowed eternal love; there I was once the happiest of mortals, and now the most miserable! Hope had left me for ever!

"I walked hurriedly forward, nor stopped on my way until I reached Purbrook; the village from whence the man had brought the letter.

Here I inquired at the inn for any particulars of the fugitives, and received information of their having started in a post-chaise for London that morning. Hunger, thirst, and the scorching heat of the sun were alike unfelt or unheeded. I started again eagerly on my way.

"I think I must have walked more than twenty miles, for I had passed Petersfield a long way, when I found my strength begin to fail me; and I threw myself down to rest on a bank at the road side; when, placing my little bundle under my head, I unconsciously fel fast asleep. The evening was just closing in as I stopped. For twenty-four hours I had neither slept, nor eaten, and had but once drunk of a spring, which I met with after leaving Purbrook.

"Nature now imperatively demanded repose; but she could not set the mind to sleep: the object of my pursuit was still before me. Fancy painted her, who I once vainly believed mine! in the hellish grasp of her seducer; and I sprang upon my feet, as I thought, to rescue her.

"It was night; all was silent as the grave; I knew not where I was, nor which way I was to go. My mind was bewildered! My limbs were stiff, and my teeth chattered with cold. I looked above—the stars were shining brilliantly, and my eye involuntarily rested upon the star *she* had once playfully called hers. It appeared to me pale, and overspread with a thin cloud. The idea aroused me, and my master-passion, revenge, coming to its assistance, effectually banished the stupor which had well nigh overwhelmed me. 'Thy star is indeed clouded,' I exclaimed aloud, ' but it shall not be my fault if the cloud be not dispersed!' And again I pursued my journey.

"Morning soon began to break, and the freshness of the air rebraced my nerves. I stopped at a little rivulet to bathe my heated temples, and found myself much renovated. I walked on until I came to a farm-house; the inmates of which were just stirring. I entered the farm-yard to procure a drink of milk; my request, made to a pretty country girl, was readily complied with; but she put me so in remembrance of the being I had lost, that I much fear my emotion overcame my thanks. I replaced the bowl on the table, and with a faltering voice, bade her good morning.

"But why should I repeat to you, my dear friend, the thousand anguished thoughts which, one after another, racked my heart? Those who have not experienced the trial, may perhaps doubt of their having existed. You will, perhaps, be inclined to blame my yielding to the torrent of my passion as I did; and I will freely own that reason formed no part of my actions. But there is a passion—you may not have felt it—yet to which all are liable, with which reason, however strong it may be in other cases, cannot cope. Such a passion inthralled—ay, still inthrals me. I have sought in gaiety, solitude, danger, and even in religion for a shield; and I have not found one able to protect me from its influence. Clara is ever present to my imagination; and though reaso whispers she has acted unworthily, my hear acknowledges *her* sovereignty alone.

"Three days I continued my journey, taking

the most scanty refreshment at any house I came to, and sleeping, sometimes in the fields, at others in some outhouse; but carefully avoiding all society. The third day I found myself in the vicinity of London—dirty, wretched, and with fifteen shillings in my pocket. It was Sunday—I went into a little public-house, and made myself as clean as my scanty wardrobe would allow me, and then, though in rather sorry plight, I walked on my way.

"As I entered London I was amazed at everything I saw. It seemed to me that all the world were keeping holiday; such crowds of well-dressed people, young and old, were thronging every path. At length I came to a beautiful bridge—it was Westminster bridge, as I afterwards heard; and all the magnificence of London, of which I had been told so much, was now, I thought, open to my view. But I could not look with delight at anything—my sight was jaundiced, and all around me appeared to be the grouping of a fantastic dream.

"Led on by chance, which had so far been my conductor, I at length, by following in the stream, found myself in a very beautiful place, which I was told was St. James's Park. Here the assemblage of beauty, pleasing scenery, and trooping of horse soldiers, made much more enchanting by the loveliness of the day, had well nigh called forth from me a burst of delight.

"Perhaps at that moment the presence of an old friend might have recalled me to a sense of my duty, and have subdued my revengeful passion to its proper bounds. But at that instant, when the balance was so nicely poised, my sight was arrested by a distant view of the parties I was in search of. I darted forward, endeavouring to gain a nearer glimpse of them; but I was only time enough to see them get into a handsome chariot, waiting at the Park gate, which immediately drove off at a rapid pace. Nothing could exceed the splendour of the lady's dress; and no one but myself would have recognised her at the distance.

"I pursued the carriage for, I suppose, a mile; I was pretty fleet, and had nearly overtaken it when it suddenly turned the corner of a street, and a number of other carriages passing at the same time, it escaped me.

"I was now in a part of the town, I knew not where, and it signified not; all parts were alike unknown to me, and unregarded. I involuntarily sauntered about the streets, and when I found myself fatigued, I went into a tavern to obtain rest.

"What a situation was mine! to what wretchedness had my obstinacy reduced me! Here was I—a stranger, and an outcast; when I ought to have been a comforter to that good soul, who was entirely alone in the world; if, indeed,—which I knew not—he was alive. But these ideas were at that time strangers to me.

"I asked to have a bed in the house, and was accommodated; and after revolving in my mind the events of the day, I dozed into a disturbed, unrefreshing sleep. The next day I inquired my way to St. James's Park—for that was the only place I knew of—in hopes of again seeing them, but without effect; and for several days I continued my visits to this place.

"At length, finding but five shillings in my pocket I began to consider my case hopeless, and resolved to retrace my steps.

"Home I had none; I, however, determined to return to Portsmouth, and if I was still unsuccessful in obtaining a meeting with Clara's seducer, volunteer to go to sea. I had no distinct plan of acting; revenge was what I burned for; all I wished was a personal *rencontre:* the rest I was willing to leave to chance.

"I had proceeded fifteen miles from London, on my return, when a postchaise overtook me; but each carriage was watched by an eye which nothing could escape. In it were the pair I had been pursuing. Clara saw me—for I heard her shriek—the rest was lost in the distance. To pursue was hopeless, and I could not afford to ride, but my strength and spirits were unabated.

"On the Monday night (having started from London on Saturday morning) I reached the village of Cosham, with an eighteenpenny piece in my pocket, and hardly any sole to my shoe. It was nearly ten o'clock, and just as I was passing a stable-yard I saw issue from thence the man I was looking for; but to be more certain, I went in and asked the hostler. I obtained from him the intelligence that the

Captain, as he called him, would return there at six o'clock in the morning for his horse.

"I had previously been sleepy, and had felt greatly fatigued. These feelings were dissipated in an instant, and I quickened my pace in hopes of overtaking him on the road. I found he was pursuing the road leading to Havant, a distance of three miles from Cosham, and although unable to come up with him, I managed to keep him in sight until he entered a small cottage near that village.

"My first idea was to go to the house and there obtain from him the satisfaction I required; but then I thought it could not be in the presence of Clara, and I determined on meeting him alone. But in order that he should not again escape me, I sat myself down at the step of the door, and there fell fast asleep: I was satisfied my prey was safe, and I slept soundly.

"I awoke soon after daylight, and looking up to the window and observing the blind down, was assured he had not escaped me. I then walked some distance down the road leading to

Cosham, and there paced to and fro, anxiously waiting for the interview.

"As I said before, I had no defined idea of my manner of acting; and now that the meeting was, as it were, within my reach, scheme after scheme was thrown aside as soon as formed, and I left my course, as before, to chance. What a tempest was raging in my heart! I had some vague notions of justice, love, and revenge, which it would be impossible to analyze. My dress was disordered, my face was dusty, dirty, and haggard, and I must have looked more like a highwayman than anything else.

"The hour at length came, and I saw him approach me. I stood still in the pathway, as firmly as if I had been rooted there. I was unobserved until he came close to me. On seeing me he started and turned pale. I stood right in his way, and firmly grasping my cudgel, sternly confronted him.

"As I seemed so determined to dispute his passage, he halted and demanded in a lofty tone, what I wanted.

"In a voice hardly articulate for anger, I replied, 'that which Lieutenant —— can hardly give me.'

"'Who, then, are you?' he said.

"'I am the avenger of Clara S——,' I answered; 'look at me again; surely you know me. Hear me, sir,' I added, 'you have stolen that poor girl from her father and me; you have ruined, and are now about to desert her! either convince me that you have married her, or let me see you marry her, or——'

"'Begone, poor fool;' he said, interrupting me, 'get out of my path;' but seeing me unmoved, he raised a weapon he had in his hand—it was a sword-stick—and struck me across the shoulder; the sword flew out with a spring and wounded me. No further provocation was required—I struck him one blow with my stick on the left temple, and he fell DEAD at my feet!

"I looked upon his senseless form, as it lay extended before me, with a kind of savage satisfaction; but I knew not then that life was extinct. Ten thousand furies possessed my breast, and I believe, had he moved a muscle, I should have repeated the blow: but he stirred not.

"At length the violence of my passion in some measure subsided, and stooping down, I unloosed his neckcloth and shirt collar, and I found suspended round his neck Clara's miniature. What a violent tumult did this occasion! I forgot everything else while gazing on the copy, the original of which I was never again to behold. I know not how long I continued looking on this quiet yet speaking picture, nor could I forbear imprinting a thousand burning kisses on the callous object.

"Finding him still insensible I began to be alarmed. I ran with haste to a little brook close by, and brought what water I could in the palms of my hands. This proving of no avail, I called to a man working in a field a short distance off, and asked him to assist me in carrying him to some place where surgical aid might be procured.

"'Lord blessee,' said the countryman, 'thou want'st a doctor too; look at thy hand, man.' I looked, and found it streaming with blood which had flowed from my shoulder.

"Fortunately, a cart was passing at the time, on the way to Cosham, the nearest place of a doctor's residence: it stopped and received the lifeless body. I begged the countryman to accompany me, as his evidence would be material, in the event of what I now began to fear—the death of my victim.

"We arrived at Cosham about half-past six, and went direct to Dr. S——, who ordered us to carry the body to a tavern opposite, and after trying, in vain, to draw blood, pronounced him a DEAD MAN!!

"With what a crushing weight did those words fall upon my heart. I, who but a few hours before had thirsted for *revenge*, now found myself *revenged* indeed!—Revenge was what I had earnestly longed for, and my wish was granted; but oh! at what a price!—I was a murderer! God forgive me! How gladly would I then have called him back to earth, and myself have taken his place in the cold arms of death. 'Happy soul!' I exclaimed, 'what bliss is yours!'

"But I was not long suffered to remain in meditation. 'Who were his murderers?' was the anxious inquiry of the surrounding people.

"'I killed him,' I answered instantly. 'I am

his murderer; and here I stand to abide the consequences.'

"The news soon flew from one end to the other of the village, that a man was murdered; and a constable being called in, I voluntarily placed myself in his custody, and resigned myself to what I considered would be an ignominious end. Death, in itself, had no terrors for me, so long as it was unaccompanied by disgrace; but the death of a criminal—oh! it was unbearable. My heart was completely subdued; all my pride, and every other feeling, was lost in the consideration that I was a murderer!

"The coroner for the county was sent for, and a jury speedily summoned. Witnesses were examined: the countryman told what he knew; and I, without the smallest reservation, told my whole story to the jury. I was obliged to bare my shoulder, which showed a deep cut; and the jury, after a long consultation, acquitted me of the crime, by a verdict of 'justifiable homicide.' They may have been right, but there was a jury within me whose verdict was more severe.

"I was liberated the same evening; but of what value was liberty to me? I was utterly reckless of everything. I drank a large glass of brandy, and then quitted the house, leaving the direction of my footsteps to chance.

"I had not gone far, before a recruiting serjeant approached me. He had been very successful; and the drums playing, ribbons flying, and the mirth of the party, had such an effect on my maddened brain, that the invitation to serve my King and country, as a loyal Marine, was unhesitatingly accepted. 'We shall start for Chatham to-morrow, my brave lad,' said he, 'after a good blow-out, which you seem to stand much in want of.' So, after passing a night, which no language can describe, I and the other recruits were placed in a waggon, hired by the serjeant, and after travelling the better part of two days, I reached Chatham more dead than alive.

"Here, as you, my kind friend, well know, I was found in a wretched plight; and to you, and your affectionate wife, whom God long spare to comfort you, I owe the continuance of my life—a mercy, I can never be sufficiently thankful to God for, since it has given me an opportunity of repenting my heinous sins. God has spared me to show me my faults in their true light; and I have sought diligently, and trust shall eventually obtain, His pardon, though I so little deserve it.

"The fever, which followed my fatigue of body and mind, kept me on the sick list for upwards of six weeks. The events which befel me when I recovered my health, it will be unnecessary to repeat; yet you must receive the only return, in addition to my never-ending gratitude, I can ever make for your kindness, and disinterested friendship, in the papers I leave you.

" Clara's fate remains to be told. After our ship was paid off, we were, as you know, sent ashore to barracks; from whence you got long leave. During that time, I could not resist the opportunity of making some inquiries concerning my old master, and his daughter.

" The little parlour wherein I used to read, had a window so low down, that a tall person could look over the blind into it. One evening, after dark, the shutters not being closed in, I was tempted to do so. There I saw my venerable master, intently reading a book I could not mistake,—it was his Bible; and there he found his only consolation. I could discover enough of his face to observe the deep worn traces of incurable sorrow—and I could look no more.

"I met with one whom I had formerly known. I was not afraid of recognition; for my Marine's clothing, and the troubles I had undergone, had so altered my features and manner, that scarcely any one would have known me. I accosted him, and asked him if he could tell me where Mr. S—— lived?

"'Yes,' he answered; 'a little way down the street.'

"I then said to him—'Do you know him?'

"'Oh, yes,' he replied, 'intimately.'

"'Well, then,' I continued, 'perhaps you will be able to answer my questions, without my troubling him, for I fear he is not altogether right, from what I have heard.'

"'He is not,' replied he. 'He never looked up after the death of his poor girl.'

"'What! and is she dead, then?' I inquired, anxiously.

"'Oh, yes,' said he, without taking any notice of my agitation; 'she has been dead these three months. But what may you want to know about them?'

"'Oh,' I returned, as carelessly as my emotion would allow me, 'I was once acquainted with the old man's prentice.'

"'What!' he said, 'Harry! Did you know Harry?—he that killed the scoundrel who ruined Clara?'

"'Yes; the same,' I replied. 'We went to the same school.'

"'Ah, poor girl,' he went on; 'she died three months back. She never held up her head, after that melancholy business, which ended in the death of her seducer, and the loss of Harry. Some people thought her mad; and I think it was enough to make her so, to lose her good name, and a faithful, kind-hearted lad, like Harry was. She lived but to throw herself at her father's feet, and ask his forgiveness, and then lay herself down and die. But the week after the news came of Harry's being killed, the cord which had bound her to life was broken,—she died in her father's arms, and 'Forgive me, Harry,' were the last words on her lips.

"I was entirely overcome; but a violent flood of tears relieved me. You know the origin of that report: it was one of the few happy days of my life—"

"Yes, I do remember it well, my poor Ned," said the serjeant, taking off his spectacles, and laying them on the table; "for although your proper name was Harry, you have no need to be ashamed of that of Ned: and I will tell you what I remember of the story—for he, poor fellow, was too brave a lad to talk much of his own battles. I gathered the account from the man whose life he so gallantly rescued.

"A few months before our return to England, we were ordered to assist some troops, in the destruction of some batteries and vessels in Diamante Bay. There were several ships, and all the Marines were sent ashore from them. I am bold to say our party was never behind-hand in these matters, and Ned was our pride.

The troops, some of whom were embarked on board our ships, and our party, landed at daybreak with little opposition, and after some hard fighting in getting to the forts, we silenced them, and entirely destroyed the shipping and gun-boats; but on mustering my party, Ned, and a young fellow who was a *chum* of his, Bill Perkins, were found to be missing. Our sorrow was very great; but it was of no use complaining; they were set down among the killed and missing, and the report to that effect was sent to England.

" About a week afterwards, to our great surprise, and joy, Ned and his comrade Perkins came alongside in a shore-boat. It appeared that in getting through the jungle before the town, Perkins had been badly wounded in the knee by a musket-ball, and had fallen. The party pushed on, and he was left with no very bright prospects before him; for he could expect nothing better than a prison, if he escaped starvation. He lay three or four hours; and at last the firing ceased. He then gave himself up for lost; as he doubted not the troops would return to the ship, and leave him to his fate.

"While he was thus meditating, three Neapolitan soldiers passed along, who had been slightly wounded, or, perhaps only frightened, and had fallen. Seeing him, one of them uttered an exclamation, as much as to say, 'here's a fine prize,' and they were proceeding to rifle his pockets—(though I think they might have spared themselves that trouble,) and made him their prisoner;—when he heard some one shouting out his name. He answered as well as he could, and he was fortunately heard, for the sound brought to his assistance Ned Cummings.

"As soon as the soldiers saw the new comer, they pointed their bayonets at him, and called on him to surrender. Ned assumed an entirely new mode of repelling a charge, and one that answered his purpose:—'He changed ends with his musket,' says Bill Perkins, 'laying hold of the barrel, and, throwing it about as if it had been a broom-stick, beat down their charge with its butt-end; and in a few minutes laid every one of them at full stretch, either dead or stunned.' Then, finding himself master of the field, he took Perkins on his back as if he had been a child, and carried him off in quick time to the sea-shore. Finding the Marines re-embarked, he took him to the quarters of the Maltese regiment, where his leg was attended to; and as he was unable to help himself, he stayed by him to nurse him. Ned was as good a nurse as a fighter, and attended him with as much care as if he had been his brother, until he was able to help himself. Now, what should you think of such a man as that?" continued the serjeant.

"I say he was a fine fellow," replied little Dick, whose tongue was longing to get loose. "Such a chap as that is worth his weight in gold!"

"It is my opinion," rejoined Peters, "that a kind-hearted man is always better than one of your bull-headed, fire-eating fellows, who see no danger, and, therefore, cannot feel any. When we find a right-down good heart, there is not much doubt about courage. True courage is made of good stuff; and you may depend upon it, that the greatest of heroes will always be found to be good and kind-hearted men. Now, I always had a good idea of Ned Cummings, although he shunned me, as he did every one else, except you,—but I never heard that account of him before; and I say, that for a man who had done his duty nobly—to leave his ranks and go in search of a wounded companion in that way, must be a right-down noble fellow."

" He was offered his discharge when the ship got to England," said the serjeant, "in consequence of that affair, and his general exemplary conduct; but he refused it."

" I can't see," said old Tim Stuart (whom one would have thought asleep during the spinning of this tough yarn, but it appears he was not—) " I can't see what harm he did, in giving that fellow, that cut his little craft out, a lick over the head: if he'd a come athwart my hawse in that way, I should have sarved him much such another trick."

" Yes, yes," replied the serjeant, "and so would most men; but still there is an article in our ' Printed Instructions,' you know, that tells us we should 'do no murder;' and that it is, you see, that troubled poor Ned. But it's my opinion that he cared less for that, than for the loss of his sweetheart: and I know by sad experience," said the serjeant with a sigh, " what it is to lose all we have set our hearts on. But come," said he, rallying, " I will just finish my story; there is not much more of it." He accordingly returned to the history.

CHAPTER IX.

"O! pale, pale now, those rosy lips,
 I oft hae kissed sae fondly!
And clos'd for ay the sparkling glance,
 That dwelt on me sae kindly."—BURNS.
 * * *
Oh! that I were where Helen lies,
Night and day on me she cries,
Out o' my bed she bids me rise;
 O come, my love, to me.
ANONYMOUS.

"I COULD no longer disguise myself from my old friend; but taking him by the hand, looked at him earnestly, and told him who I was. He gazed on me with astonishment. 'It *is* Harry, indeed,' he said, seizing my hand; 'but I applied for you constantly at the barracks, by the request of your old master, and the last time, when informed of your death, was assured of your being the man, by being shown your assumed name in a copy of the official return, and by the date of the enlistment; as well as by a letter received from Chatham, stating the ship you were embarked in. Your poor old master loved you as his child; and when I told him of your death, I thought I had caused his. —And poor Clara—'

"'Say no more, I pray,' I said, interrupting him. 'I cannot bear it now; but tell me where she is buried. I must kiss the ground that covers her, and then return to seek for the death that I have as yet sought for in vain from my country's enemies.'

"My old friend endeavoured, with all the warmth of early friendship, to induce me to return to my master, and forego my profession; but without moving me. He said everything to turn me. He pointed out the comfort I should be able to administer to him, who was now without a single earthly tie; and if any argument could have prevailed, this would have done so. But my determination to devote my life to my country's service, to which I was now become used, and the immovable heart within me, rendered his persuasions unavailing.

"I bound him over, with some difficulty, to keep the fact of my being alive secret; and, having obtained some direction for the grave, I went the next evening to the country churchyard, at Kingston. I had not much difficulty in finding the spot, as, from the description, it was not far from the tomb which contains the remains of some of the men, who were drowned by the sinking of the Royal George at Spithead.

"As I approached the grave of Clara, and of my affections, all the love I had ever felt returned upon me as a torrent, which I could not withstand. I threw myself on the grassy mound that covered her earthly remains, and invoked a prayer for her eternal happiness.

"At the head of the grave was a stone, on which was engraved the few and simple words that best befit the occasion,—her name, age, and time of her departure. I traced each letter of her name, and it brought the past full before me. I felt that I had nothing to forgive, for I had never suffered my heart to vent a thought against her; but now that she was beyond the reach of reproach—now that I saw the spot which inclosed her remains—I cursed my own obstinacy, which had brought her to a premature end.

"I lived the last few years over again in my mind. I asked myself what was her crime? She had listened to the voice of a man of the world. He had told her she was born to be an ornament to society, and not the humble wife of a tradesman. He styled himself a man of rank and affluence—he promised her a carriage to ride in, and servants to attend her—he told her, her beauty was sufficient to command all these fine things;—she listened,—and what was *I* to such inducements as these? He told her I was a *poor printer's boy*. Think of this, and condemn her not—condemn rather human nature.

"Of all the taunts to which woman is subject, none are so keenly felt as those of ridicule. Had he told her I was poor, she would have loved me the better. Had he attempted to defame my character,—throw imputations on my behaviour,—spoken of the inconveniences of a contracted income, he had failed; her love would have laughed at these things. But a sarcasm, a sneer, when truth could be brought to its aid, was too much. I *was* a poor printer's boy; but this truth was too powerful a weapon for Clara, when wielded sarcastically by a cunning and designing adversary. He thus obtained a hold on her mind—she wavered—she fell—she fell not UNREVENGED: but it added nothing to her peace.

"Hours passed, and still I remained on the grave of all I ever loved: I felt transfixed to the spot. Darkness came on, I was still seated in the same posture. I ransacked the treasury of my memory, wherein were stored all the little incidents of the happy days, which were, alas! flown for ever. I thought of her artlessness—her virtue—and her fall;—and full of these reflections, I leaned back against the head-stone, and fell into a kind of stupor.

"Imagination was still busy. I thought she appeared before me arrayed in white; and her loveliness seemed greater, if possible, than when living. She took me by the hand. I recall the thrilling sensation of her touch. I rose, and she led me to the church. A large party were in attendance, all gaily dressed, and I fancied myself also in the attire of a bridegroom. The church doors were open; we walked forward to the altar; the priest opened his book; again I looked at him—it was the ghastly form of *death!* The horror of the dream aroused me. It was quite dark—the sky seemed one black cloud. My dream—it must have been my dream—returned upon me.

"There stood Clara before me: there she was just as my dream had pictured her; lovely, as my fondest fancy had ever beheld her. Her attitude was one of sorrow, and for a time I was paralysed. At length I rushed forward to clasp the phantom in my arms, and it instantly vanished. I am not naturally superstitious; but if ever the mortal form of a deceased person visited an inhabitant of earth, Clara appeared to me.

"I sank down again on her grave: I earnestly prayed for death, and that one grave might inclose us both. The remembrance of my calling, however, restored me to a sense of my duty;

and I tore myself from the hallowed spot; which I often afterwards visited.

"Once since that time she has appeared to me. It was only a few nights since. I was sentry on the poop of the hulk, in the middle watch. Perhaps my mind was still full of the dream in the churchyard; but the same form crossed my path three several times, and the third time she held up a ring, and, beckoning me to follow her, vanished from my sight. There is a something within me which tells me, that the day is not far distant which will eternally unite us.

"Farewell! my old and sincere friend—may the Giver of all good things reward you for your kindness to me! I leave you the little I possess. The accompanying documents will, I have no doubt, put you in possession of my arrears of prize-money, and any thing else which may be due to me. I cannot explain the presentiment I have of my never again leaving England; but it is a feeling I cannot shake off; yet it shall never, while reason holds her seat, be by my own hand. It has often occurred to me, to end by some such act the troubles of my life; but I have scorned the cowardly thought; and my religion has taught me its sin. My life was given me by my God, and it shall be endured during His pleasure. In the words of my old master's favourite I can say,—

> "'Henceforth I fly not death, nor would prolong
> Life much, bent rather how I may be quit,
> Fairest and easiest, of this cumbrous charge,
> Which I must keep till my appointed day
> Of rendering up, and patiently attend
> My dissolution.'"

"It is my wish to die in fighting my country's battles; and for that reason I have refused my discharge. My present employment, though unsuitable to my habits, is less so than any other would be; for here my thoughts are not intruded upon.

"And now I once more bid you farewell! for by the time you read this I shall be in another, and I fear not, a better world. I never intended the death of any one; and for the crimes I committed I have diligently sought, and I trust shall obtain, pardon. God bless you! "H. D."

"Such is the end of the manuscript," continued the serjeant, "and the following letter was the one he alluded to when he gave me the packet. It was addressed to Mr. S.; but as the ship sailed without giving me an opportunity of complying with the request that I would present it myself, I was obliged to keep it, until I again returned to England. In the meantime the old gentleman died. It runs thus:—

"'My ever honoured Master.—Death will ave ended my wretched career ere this letter reaches you. But I cannot leave you for ever, without craving that pardon to my memory, which I have never asked to my life. My rime against you is one of black ingratitude. You were more than my father—to you I was indebted for everything in me that was praiseworthy. You taught me to contemn all that was evil, and revere all that was good. But a cloud overshadowed me: some monstrous demon took possession of my heart, and ingratitude to my God and to you was his attribute. The future appears now to me as one dark mass, yet at times I seem to pierce through it, and discover another, and a far better, country. It is there I hope to join the soul which still draws mine to it;—it is there my highly wrought fancies picture a blissful meeting,—when we, disburdened of this mortal coil, shall mingle in unalloyed purity. Something whispers 'peace' to me. I have asked forgiveness of my God. My stubbornness was hard to overcome, but was at length subdued; and the heart which man could not soften, God has melted. The blood which is upon my head is a grievous weight; but I fervently thank God, I never intended *his* death. I thought to avenge your wrongs; yet I sought that revenge which belongs not to man. A presentiment comes over me that, in a few days, I shall be the habitant of other regions. The time which remains to me shall be employed, as much as possible, in preparation for the change; and in the prayers I make, you, who I have never yet forgotten, will be still remembered.—Adieu.

"'August 18, 18—.'

"We had left the harbour," said the serjeant, "and were at anchor at Spithead, expecting to sail the next morning at daybreak for the East India station. Advance had been paid; and, in order to prevent desertion, three sentries were planted; one in each gangway, and one on the poop; and in addition, the officer of marines was ordered to keep the first, and I, the middle watch. Ned had the middle watch also, and was stationed in the larboard gangway.

"I had the morning before taken leave of my fond wife and child; and debased indeed must be the heart, which does not feel the anguish of such a separation. As might be expected, I was very low spirited. I did not enter into conversation with Ned—it would not have been right; but, as I gave him his orders, I thought he looked unusually pale.

"The night was very sultry and pitchy dark, but occasionally illumined, by vivid flashes of sheet lightning: there was hardly a breath of wind.

"There is, to the thinking mind, a great solemnity in the quiet which reigns during a middle watch, throughout a ship when at anchor; and this melancholy watch was accompanied with everything to cause gloom:—each man seemed wrapt in his own meditations; and all things conspired to produce on my mind a feeling of utter desolation.

"It had just struck three bells, when I observed Cummings looking very anxiously over the gangway; and, going to him, I asked him if he saw anything.

"'Yes,' he replied hurriedly; 'and don't you see that boat, yonder, lying on her oars?' and then in a firm tone he called out—'Boat a-hoy!'

"'I cannot see any boat,' I said. He, however, appeared quite certain that there was one; and a bright flash of lightning seemed to confirm him in the opinion.

"'There,' he exclaimed wildly; 'don't you see her now?' and stretching out, as if intently gazing at something, and trying to gain a nearer view, he vanished in an instant. There was a sullen plunge in the water, and looking over the side, he had disappeared entirely, without a struggle. He sank like a stone, and not a vestige of him was ever, that I heard of, found.

"The cry of 'a man overboard!' was quickly heard.

"'Keep a good look-out, sentries,' said the officer of the watch, 'and fire at any boat you see! Boatswain's-mate, pipe the first cutter away—aft there and lower the boat down—bear a hand!' The boat's crew having been ordered to be ready, in case of being wanted—a very prudent precaution — had the boat lowered down, and alongside in a few minutes, and the mate of the watch—you know who I mean, Peters—was ordered to row round the ship, to see what had become of the man. No trace of him was however discovered; and, after rowing about for half an hour, the boat returned.

"And do you think he intended to drown himself?" asked Peters, interrupting the serjeant's narrative.

"Certainly not," replied the serjeant. "I was convinced it was accidental, before I knew anything of the memoir he gave me; and after reading that, the thought strikes me that a recurrence of the phantom of the brain, which he has spoken of, caused him to believe he saw something; and that, in his anxiety to see it yet clearer, he overbalanced himself and fell overboard. The sentry on the poop told some out-of-the-way story about the matter; and thus, out of a simple accident, the report was circulated round the ship, that Ned Cummings had been carried off in a flash of lightning."

"That fellow told me," said Peters, "that he saw a boat on the larboard beam, and that there was a white lady standing up in it; and he swore to it so positively, that I for a long time considered Ned Cummings had jumped overboard, in hopes of being able to desert, and make his escape by swimming to the boat. But your account soon convinced me to the contrary; and I now agree with you, that the ghost of his sweetheart called him to her."

"Or," added the serjeant, "his weak brain made him think so."

"And why not a real ghost?" said old Tim Stuart. "You don't mane to say there aint none, do you?"

"I will never believe in such things until I see one myself," answered the serjeant.

"No more would I," returned Tim; "but I

have seen one; and if you don't believe in
ghosts after what I am going to tell you, why,
I say you won't believe in nothing. It's a
great many years agone now; for I was then a
young fellow, and second captain of the fore-
top, and now I am an old buffer, almost
seventy. I belonged to a smart frigate in the
East Indies, and she was lying at anchor in
Madras roads. If I'd a-ben at all in liquor,
you might have thought as how I couldn't see
clear; but I wasn't. I might have been cook
of the mess, but I was no more drunk than I
am now.

"'Cause it was so hot on the lower deck,
and I couldn't sleep, I roused out, shoved on
my trousers, took my monkey-jacket for a
pillow, and went up on the forecastle, and
thought to caulk it out. But somehow, though
I pricked for the softest plank, I couldn't get a
wink of sleep; so I bundled up my traps, and
shifted my berth a second time, and at last
found a snug berth on the booms, under the
bow of the launch, and got off to sleep. Well
—I hadn't been asleep long afore a something

touched me on the forehead, as it might be, so —(touching his forehead)—as gentle as may be, but it waked me directly. I opened my eyes, (for I had two at that time) but didn't move my head—and close alongside of me, there stood a young chap, a townsman of mine, a nice young fellow, by the name of Tom Green.

"So, says I to him, 'what are you after, Tom?' says I; 'when did you come aboard?' for I thought he was away in the jolly-boat —for she was away from the ship, waiting outside the surf for some of the officers as was expected off. With that he lifted up the stump of one arm, and showed it to me, bleeding, just as if his hand had been shot off; and as I was going to ask him how it happened, he vanished away all at once.

"So I thought he had gone down the fore-ladder into the waist, and I tried to get up, to go down after him, and forgetting the boat above my head, I almost stove in my skull. But I got up, nevertheless, and down I went, but he wasn't there; and I heard a boat alongside, so I went on deck to the gangway, thinking it might be the jolly-boat, and it was.

"I waited till one of the crew came up, to see about young Tom Green—for Tom was a chum of mine; and when the coxen came up the side, says I to him, 'what's the matter, Jim?' for I saw he looked a little queer.

"'Why,' says he, 'we've a-lost Tom Green.'

"'Lost Tom!' says I; 'how so?'

"'Why,' says he, 'I'll tell you. While we was a-waiting, just paddling with the oars, to keep outside the surf, a something unshipped our rudder, and the lanyard wasn't fast,—we thinks now that a shark gave it a slap with his fin,—and so we backed water until it come alongside, and Tom reached over the gunwale to lay hold of it, and haul it inboard; when all at once he sung out—'A shark! a shark!' and, before we could help him, a shark had got hold of his hand, and hauled him over the side, and we saw no more of him.'

"Now, what do you say to that? You can't say it wasn't Tom's ghost as I saw. Why he stood afore me as plain as I ever see him in my life—and then, you know, he was in the shark's maw."

"It is very strange," said the serjeant, who

was evidently still sceptical. "How long had the boat been alongside before you went to the gangway?"

"Only just time enough for the officers to get out," replied Tim. "And why shouldn't the young man as you have been reading about have seen his sweetheart's ghost, as well as for me to see young Tom Green's?"

"Well," answered the serjeant, "when I see one I'll believe, and not before. So, good night, my lads, and I hope you have been amused with my story."

"Yes, very much indeed," answered the wakeful part of the community; but by far the greater part had been a long time fast asleep, and were only awakened by its cessation.

The party now wished each other good night, and separated.

CHAPTER X.

> Ha! who comes here?
> I think it is the weakness of mine eyes
> That shapes this monstrous apparition.
>
>   SHAKS. *E.*

"TALKING about ghosts," said our friend the serjeant, on one evening a short time after the scene just related, "did you ever hear me tell of the ghost I saw some years ago, when I first went to sea?"

"No; but I should like to hear it very much," replied old Tim, who was always curious in such matters.

"Why, soon after I enlisted," said the serjeant, "I was drafted into the Old Lion, sixty-four, nearly forty years back. I was then about nineteen, and did not know quite so much of those matters as I do now.

"The carpenter of the ship, old Mr. Hawkington, fell sick one day, and after a short illness died. He was a man very much respected on board, and every one was sorry for him. As the ship was ordered into port, where we expected to arrive in a few days, the captain allowed him to be kept, so that he might be buried on shore; and a sentry was placed, as usual, over the cabin door in the cockpit. The old gentleman had been dead three or four days, I do not rightly remember which; but as contrary winds had kept us out longer than we expected, it was decided that he should be committed to the deep on the following day.

"It so happened that I was sentry over the dead body, the night before it was to have been buried; but so far from my being given to foolish superstitious fears—"

"Not so foolish, I can tell you," interjected old Tim.

"Well, well," said the serjeant, "I would not have thought much of passing a night in a church or a church-yard, as I have done many a time, and in no very pious company either; or in a haunted chamber, or anything in that way. But we do not, any of us, know our weakness or strength until we are tried."

" That's true," said old Tim again.

" In this instance," continued the serjeant, " my nerves were put to a very severe trial. It was just past two bells in the middle watch. I I was walking to and fro, thinking about one thing and 'tother; sometimes of my wife, that I had left at home; but, at any rate, of anything more than about the dead body I was sentry over, because I was quite satisfied there was no danger of his deserting.

" My lanthorn was hanging to a beam, through the discoloured horn of which a purser's dip was throwing a very poor light, and I stopped to endeavour to improve it by snuffing, or lighting a new candle, as might be necessary.

" While I was thus employed, not having quite finished my job, the door of the dead man's cabin was thrown back with a loud bang, which could only have been effected by a very powerful hand, and I distinctly heard a gruff, hollow voice roar out, 'Give us a light, sentry!' The horrid voice and noise so startled me, that I clutched hold of the lanthorn—when the nail on which it was hung gave way—the lanthorn fell from my grasp, the light was extinguished, and with two long strides and a spring I reached the upper step of the cockpit ladder.

"That which had given such agility to my limbs seemed to have fettered my tongue, and I stood at the top of the ladder, gasping for breath, without the power of saying a word. A sort of cold sweat was on my forehead, and my hat rose several inches from my head, elevated by the mutinous conduct of every hair, notwithstanding the powder and pomatum, which at other times kept them in subjection.

"How long these effects lasted I cannot exactly say; but they were in no degree lessened by hearing strange noises issuing from below, as if some one was moving about, and growling, swearing, and talking to another person. At length the noises, and some rather heavy footsteps approached the foot of the ladder whereon I had been standing for some considerable time, without moving hand or foot.

"It now appeared to me only prudent to move on, and I accordingly walked a little forward on the lower deck. I had sufficient courage to look behind me, and I distinctly saw— it's quite true, I assure you—I distinctly saw, as plain as I see you now—"

"I believes you," said Tim, in whose countenance the most painful interest was manifest.

"The ghost!" continued the serjeant, "that is, the tall, gaunt figure of the carpenter. He was near seven feet high, I'm sure, rising slowly up out of the cockpit, and then he walked forward after me. So I walked faster, and so did Mr. Hawkington's ghost; I went up the fore ladder, and the ghost followed me; so I walked aft, and it seemed I doubled upon the apparition, for I saw it go up the ladder on to the forecastle."

"And did the men on the forecastle see it too?" asked Tim eagerly.

"O yes," answered the serjeant. "The weather was warm, and the watch on deck were lying about the forecastle and gangways, some asleep, and some looking at the moon, that was shining as bright as could be. The ghost appeared to take no notice of any of them, but took the walk the old gentleman, Mr. Hawkington, was accustomed to take when alive, and still kept his hands behind him, and his chin upon his breast, like as if he was deep in thought.

"So presently one of the men makes him out, and he roused his nearest watchmate, and pointed out the ghost to him, saying, 'I say, Tom, I'm blest if there ain't the old carpenter! here he comes—I shall be off,' and he got up and walked aft. The whisper went the rounds rapidly, and in a few minutes the forecastle was as clear as if it had been raining, or the men had heard the pipe, 'wash decks,' and the carpenter's ghost had it all to himself."

"Did any body speak to it?" asked Tim again.

"You shall hear presently," said the serjeant.

"'What do you all want here?' said the officer of the watch to the men, as they crowded aft to the quarter-deck. No one seemed inclined to answer this question at first; but on the question being repeated, accompanied with an order for them to go forward again, the captain of the forecastle, a sturdy old tar, who used to say 'he would sooner face the devil himself any time than his ghost,' muttered something about the carpenter's ghost.

"'What! What's that you say?' asked the lieutenant.

"'The carpenter's ghost! the carpenter's ghost!' reiterated half a dozen voices at once.

"'What about the carpenter's ghost, you blockheads?' replied the lieutenant; 'be off forward, and don't be stopping up the gangway in this manner.'

"'He's walking the forecastle!' exclaimed the men, still keeping their station, notwithstanding the orders of the officer of the watch.

"'Nonsense, men, nonsense!' said the officer; "Mr. Hawkington's dead; I am astonished at you'

"'He is walking the forecastle *now*, Sir,' again urged one of the half dozen of voices.

"' He has got on the very same hat as I covered for him,' rejoined another.

"' And the same old monkey-jacket,' added a third.

"' With the end of the chalk line hanging out of his pocket,' continued a fourth.

"' Only go forward and see,' exclaimed a fifth.

"' Parcel of fools!' said the lieutenant, enraged; ' make a lane there, and let me go forward.' A lane was speedily made, and the lieutenant went on very boldly until he got to the bow of the barge, and there, sure enough, as the men had said, he saw the apparition taking his ease, walking slowly backwards and forwards. The lieutenant's courage then began to fail him—"

" I don't wonder at that," said Tim.

" And he did not think it prudent to go any nearer," continued the serjeant.

" I thought how it would turn out," said Tim again.

"So he stood still at the bow of the boat," resumed the serjeant, "and after a great effort, be managed to call out, ' M-i-s-t-e-r H-a-w-k-i-n-g-t-o-n i-s i-s i-s i-s tha-tha-tha-t yo-you?'

"'Sir,' replied the apparition, raising his head."

"The devil he did!" exclaimed Tim.

"Yes," continued the serjeant, "and he touched his hat, and advanced towards the lieutenant. 'Tha-tha-t will d-do, M-i-s-t-e-r Hawk-Hawk-Hawking-ton,' ejaculated the perfectly satisfied lieutenant, retreating a few steps as the ghost advanced, as though unwilling to lessen the distance between them; and he walked very briskly aft to the quarter-deck, and went into the captain's cabin, to report the remarkable circumstance to the captain.

"'The carpenter is on the forecastle, sir,' said the lieutenant to the captain. The captain, just awaked out of a sound sleep, did not appear to hear what was said.

"'Well, sir,' responded the captain, rubbing his eyes, and waiting further particulars.

"'Mr. Hawkington, sir, is walking the deck, sir," said the lieutenant again.

"'Oh, is that all, sir?' said the captain turning himself in his cot and resuming his slumbers, 'then, sir, let him walk, and be ——.'

"It appears," continued the serjeant, "that the old carpenter had been all the time in a trance; the doctor only considered him dead—"

"Pshaw!" exclaimed the mortified Old Tim, who evidently had not made up his mind to such a conclusion; "and so it was no ghost after all?"

"No, no," replied the serjeant appeasingly. "He came to his senses in time to prevent being drowned. It seems he was quite unmindful of the time which had passed away, and waking and hearing two bells strike, he thought it was in the morning watch, and time for him to turn out; and so he roused out, called for a light as usual, fumbled about and found his clothes, and giving a curse or two to me for putting out the light, *bundled on deck as was his custom.*"

CHAPTER XI.

> " Prepare
> To see the life as lively painted, as ever
> Still sleep mocked death."—SHAKSPEARE.

"You spin a very fine yarn, no doubt, Mr. Jim," said our little fat friend, Dick Slender, who was an attentive listener; "but I can tell you we got a new hand coming amongst us, to fill up No. 10 cabin, as I'll back against you any day."

"I am very glad to hear it," replied the serjeant, "for I love to hear a good story as well as any body."

"And he's just the chap as can give it you," rejoined Dick. "I remember Young Charley—that's Old Charley now, you know, 'cause it is a matter of thirty years back, and he knowed how to get double 'lowance of grog any day, out of any mess all round the lower deck. He was a messmate of mine, and I never seed his match at singing a song, or spinning a yarn as long and as tough as the main-top-bow-line, as 'ud last out a four-hours' watch, and make it seven bells afore you hardly knowed the watch had a been called. And here he comes to speak for himself," said he, getting up off the bench, and waddling like a duck in a gutter, to meet the above-mentioned hero, who just then made his appearance. Seizing him by the hand, he exclaimed, "Glad to see you, Charley, with all my heart! and there aint no better ward than this here in the house. Come along and shake hands with your wardmates (as fine a set of chaps as you'd wish to see)," added he in a kind of whisper. So saying, little Fat Jack took hold of Charley's hand, and conducted him to the men assembled round the fire, much after the fashion of a gentleman leading his fair partner to the supper table.

The whole, with the one exception of the stationary Toby, got up to salute their new wardmate, with all the warmth of heart so natural to them; each giving his horny hand a friendly shake.

"Young Charley"—or "Old Charley" as Dick Slender justly remarks he ought now to be called,—would have suited well as a model for a sculptor, or painter, of a Telamonian Ajax; since, added to a frame which was six feet two in height, his skin appeared to be quite impervious to all attacks, whether of warfare or weather. Charley's countenance was full of good nature, yet his brows overhung his eyes, and almost shaded them from view. His voice was of the deepest bass, and his actions, conversation, and good servitude, marked him down as a genuine British sailor of the old school.

By this is not meant, a man whose pretensions are based upon a pig-tail as thick as your wrist, long ringlets, low crowned hat, and white duck trowsers very wide at the bottom; but on the contrary, a man despising these fopperies, (long since transferred to the Yankees,) and whose claims to that title rest upon firmness in action and dutiful demeanour; and who, though occasionally merrier than usual, is careful to keep his convivialities for proper times and seasons.

"Have a drop of hospital-beer, Charley?" asked little Dick, bringing out his bottle, and tendering him some of that homely beverage.

"No, no," answered the old man, rejecting the proffered draught; "none o' your belly wengeance for me, but I'll ha' a drop of rum if you like."

"A drop of rum!" exclaimed Little Dick, looking up with much surprise at the request: "why it wants only two days to pay-day, and where should we get rum? It's not much of that stuff you'll get here, old boy."

"Why, I think it would only be right," said Tim Stuart, "to welcome our new wardmate with a bottle of rum; but most of us has clean-swept holds I'm thinking."

"Well," said the serjeant, "here's my part towards it; and try and see how much we can muster amongst us, if it's only for the *honor of the ward*, you know."

"I wish Tom Peters was here," said Fat Jack: "'cause he always pays for me." But as Tom was not present, it became necessary that a general overhaul of pockets should take place; for they could none of them resist the force of the appeal made to them by the serjeant.

When the *honor of the ward* was at stake, not one of them would have thought of withholding his best services. A ward with a bad name is almost universally shunned and disliked, and a thief, or notoriously bad character, every one will do his utmost to get turned out. But as the honor of the —— ward is now only concerned, so far as it relates to its name for hospitality, it would hardly be fair to digress from the subject, to relate traits foreign to the subject.

Old Toby was roused with difficulty from his lethargic state, and told to deliver up his money; but as he stated his insolvency, it became necessary that the contents of his pockets should be made public. A general search took place therefore; and first there made their appearance, a number of old prize certificates, doubled, backed and sewn, wrapped up in a piece of white-brown paper, and bearing sundry initials and remarks on them, by which it was evident they had been frequently presented at the prize office, for the recovery of sums imagined to be due on them. In the next place, there was a steel tobacco-box, very bright from its constant wear. As this is a common depositary for money, it was deemed necessary to open it; but in addition to a small quantity of *neger head* in its pure state, and a small quantity *not* in its pure state—the box exhibited nothing of value. Then there was a short pipe also in the pocket, a pair of spectacles deficient one glass, an old clasp knife rolled round with a greasy lanyard, and to crown the whole, a halfpenny!

Tim Stuart next submitted to the right of search, and amongst his valuables there were found two farthings, and a sixpence with a hole in it; which latter Tim refused to part with, saying it was a lucky one, and that it had been in his possession many years, even when he was near dying for want of tobacco, or a glass of rum.

Fat Jack's pockets produced three halfpence;

but Jerry, the handsome little fellow described at such length in the first chapter, pleaded his wife; at the same time making the following curious disclosures, respecting his way of spending his money:

"I gits ony three shillings on pay-days," (every two weeks), "and out of that I pays a shilling a week for a room for my old 'oman, and sixpence for tea and sugar; then I has to buy firing, and all that, out of the rest: and vat can you 'spect to get out o' me? Never any of you get married!" added the little man, with much sincerity in his manner. "I could do well enough if it wa'dnt that I has to keep the old girl; for she has a wery good appetite, and my allowance aint much ven you comes to make it feed two."

He was proceeding to give more of this valuable advice, when the welcome thump! thump! of a wooden leg on the stairs, betokened the arrival of Tom Peters.

"Ah, here comes the jolly good fellow. Hurra! my lads," exclaimed Little Dick Slender; at the same time returning to his pocket a sixpence, which he had previously, though apparently unwillingly, drawn out, for the purpose of adding it to the subscription; and most of the others following his advice, also suspended payment.

Tom advanced towards the party with a magisterial air, of which he could not altogether divest himself; and Little Dick rose to introduce to him in all due form, the new comer. "Tom," said he, "here is a right down good-one come among us, and one of the true breed,—none o' your half and half picked-up-along-shore sort: shake hands with him, Charley."

Tom looked at Charley, and Charley at Tom for some moments, as if they each gazed on features they had before known; and as if their minds were revolving strange scenes long past; at the end of which pause, without a word spoken on either side, each grasped the other's hand, with the firmness of old and earnest friendship.

"Why, if it is not old Charley Wilson, I am a Dutchman!" said Tom, giving his hand another squeeze.

"Yes, Mr. Peters, here's his hulk come to take up his moorings in the Greenwich tier. But how comes you here? I thought you was one of them gentlemen sort of fellows, as cuts about in their coaches?"

"It is a long story, Charley, and meanwhile I should like to know something about you; but come and sit down, for a cold night like this, makes a fire-side a pleasant place."

Again, and again, did these veterans scan each other's features, watching the ravages time and care had made on them; and often, while the full orbed drops collected and glistened in their eyes, did their hands unite in the warm grasp of affection. It was evident that their's was a friendship of no ordinary kind.

Meanwhile little Dick rubbed his hands, and chuckled to himself, at what he knew would be forthcoming; Toby suspended his snoring for a time; Old Tim Stewart wiped his mouth; and Little Jerry obsequiously tendered his services on the occasion. The serjeant participated in the delight apparent in Tom's countenance, and the dim light thrown from the suspended lamp, deducting very little from the cheerful blaze of the fire, gave to their furrowed cheeks an increased glow, and formed an excellent subject for a Wilkie.

In a short time afterwards, Jerry was seen unlading his pocket of a large case bottle, which he had procured for the edification and amusement of the party; and very soon afterwards, each of them were trying the virtues of " Old Hawkins's best."

" Well, my old companion," said Tom to his newly found old friend, "and how many years is it since you and I sailed together?"

" Nigh hand five-and-twenty, Mr. Peters— "

" None of your misters, Charley; I am no mister now; all alike here—no difference; drop all about misters," said Tom, interrupting him.

" I don't think we have met since the ' Blue-eyed Nancy'—ah! them was the days, Captain! —that was a smart little thing, that, as ever was put together."

" Ah, no more Nancy, or Nantz either," said Tom ; "those days are all gone past."

" You tipped some of the sharp-shooters the

double now and then though, captain," returned Charley, who did not seem inclined to drop the subject, "and I thought you was a rich man by this time. But, then, its all one, captain—can't always have a fair wind and smooth water; but when I thinks of that little Nancy, and what a dance I led the cutter when she chased me, and me all by myself, it makes me a young man again. I should like to have another touch at it; but it's all up,—not a tub to be run or a box of lace. Why, captain," continued the old man, who had evidently got his jawing tacks aboard, "I've been going on fifty-six years at sea, man and boy; thirty-six year in a man-of-war, five year of that for the Blue-eyed Nancy. Ah! we ought to have got away that time, sir—that is, captain."

"Call me Tom for shortness, Charley," said Peters.

"Well, Tom, then," said Charley, "but all's one," taking a long pull at his grog. "Thirty-six year in a man-of-war is a good spell, only I run three times, and they only gives me sixteen year good sarvitude. And then I've been in a marchantman, three voyages in East *Ingeemen*, and done a little in the privateer line, and once took a passage in a pirate; five times cast away, three times in French prison; and here I am, you see, brought up at last,—so here's to better luck, shipmates! Dick, here's to you my lad, and a fair wind to them as wants one,"—when, disdaining to leave a drop in the bowl after such a toast, he drank it off to the dregs.

CHAPTER XII.

——"Where I could not be honest
I never yet was valiant."—SHAKSPEARE.

"COME, fill up again, my old boy," said Tom: "and now I think of it, tell us how you managed to give the cutter such a dodging, after we left you drunk in the lee scuppers."

"No, no, captain," replied Charley, "not drunk, only a little fresh. Well, well, if you had stayed by the craft, and knock'd the revenue men over-board, you might ha' run her to this time. Why, look'ee, shipmates, the Blue-eyed Nancy was a fine fast little thing, built at Itchen—that's the place for cutter-building. Give her a double-reefed mainsail, and let me see the craft as would overhaul her on a wind! No grog at that work, my lads—no, devil the drop; splice the main-brace out of the scuttle-butt as often as you liked; and you might have plenty of prime stuff too. But though I thinks it good, and likes it, I never used to touch it; 'cause you see, if I once got my mouth to a bottle, it stuck there; and so I knowed myself better than to try it. Here's to you all, shipmates,"—taking another long and strong pull at his rum and water.—Not much of the latter.

"But how came you, then, to be in the lee scuppers when we left her that morning?" asked Peters.

"Ah! that's like you, captain. You knows I had a touch of the lumbago, and I took a small drop of the Skeedam, just to keep out the cold and the fog, and that's how it was; and then it sent me to sleep, and when I got up there I was all by myself. But as I was going to tell you——here's your health, captain——we sailed from Cherbourg, one night just afore dark, with a slashing breeze at S.E.,—three hundred—yes, that was it—three hundred tubs in—and I had a box or so of lace on my own account, 'cause, you see, I was going to be spliced."

"And a werry good thing you wa'snt, Mr. Charley," gravely murmured Jerry.

"May be, may be, my Briton; there's many a good run has been knocked up by the women's tongues, and I sometimes thinks that Miss Kitty got talking about the fine things I was going to bring her, and somebody heerd her and laid the *infamation*. She married a butcher. I'd a' spoilt the look of his sheep's head if I'd a' come athwart him. But as to the matter of the cruise, you see, it was just as this—just as we got off the Bill, the wind all died away, and it comed on thick and foggy— month of November, you see."

"Now," said Tom, interrupting him, "as you thought proper to take your medicine for the lumbago——"

"And to keep out the fog, captain; finest thing in the world," added Charley.

"—So that you dont take too much of it," continued Peters, "as you did, and when I made your number I could'nt find you. But this is how it was, Charley, and I will tell you all about it. Soon after the fog came on so thick, it was about six o'clock in the morning,

I think, and a dead calm, I heard the sound of oars, and knew in a minute that some galley was at hand. I had ten men, you know, famous fellows, all Isle of Wight men, and brave lads too, but I always told them I did not want them to fight against the laws; if we could run a cargo now and then, well and good; but I would not allow any shooting at the revenue men, because they only did their duty.

"So I called the men, and told them how to act when the galley got alongside. I ordered them to lay down, and if the galley boarded us, to jump up when I gave the signal, seize the men, and then we could try to make our escape, if it came to the worst, in the boat. So I took the tiller, and the galley came under the vessel's quarter and hailed—

"'What vessel's that?'

"'The Ann,' said I.

"'Where are you from?'

"'Why,' I answered, 'as I suppose you wont take my word, you had better come and see.' They hesitated a moment, and then pulling sharp up alongside, out jumped five of the crew, cutlass in hand, upon our deck.

"As soon as I saw that they were intending to board, I ran forward, and saying, 'Now, my lads!' My crew sprang up, and, regardless of a few slashes, succeeded in overpowering the boarders, when they were bound hand and foot. One man remained in the galley, but half-a-dozen pistols pointed at his head induced him to come out, and submit to the same restraint as the rest.

"Having so far succeeded, it remained to be seen what chance we had of getting away. I soon, however, discovered by the burning of blue lights, that the galley's cutter was not far off, and in shore of me. I then told the men that we must make a start. We, therefore, got up a few light things, and put them into the galley, and taking with me my rifle among other valuables, we shoved off, leaving the 'Blue-eyed Nancy' to her fate.

"The galley was a six-oared boat; and as there were ten of us altogether, and as another would very likely have led to the capture of the whole, the men did not give themselves much trouble about you, and as you did not choose to look out for yourself, we left you to take care of the craft."

"While you took care of yourselves," said Charley, rather grumpishly — " but you only sarved me right, I own that."

"So we hauled up the fore-sheet and shoved off," continued Tom. "The firing of muskets, and burning of blue lights on board the cutter, served very well to show me how to give her a wide berth. After pulling about an hour, steering by compass, I had the mortification, as the day broke, to see the fog disperse; and in a short time the cutter made us out, and despatched her remaining galley in chace of us. As, however, we had a good start, I was in no fear at first for her, altho' we had about seven miles to pull.

"But our galley was very heavy, and to my great concern, I found the boat astern coming up with us hand over hand. My men pulled as might be expected when their stake was so great, but she was evidently going three feet to our two, and therefore neared us rapidly. I cheered the men up as well as I could, by telling them we *would* not be taken, and they knew I generally said what I meant."

"That's true, Captain!" exclaimed Charley.

"So soon as the cutter's boat got within hail, I stood up in the stern sheets of the galley, and hailed her to keep off. The officer in the boat replied by calling upon me to surrender; and, as I would not do that, he ordered one of his men to favour me with a shot: which was done, the man discharging two or three muskets at me, one after another.

"I then took up my rifle, as I did not like to be shot at for nothing, and taking aim at the boat's bow, I fired: the ball struck her between wind and water, making a long diagonal hole on both sides the stem. I then took up a musket, and firing again, the shot struck her under the bilge, making another hole, equally unpleasant to them; then wishing them 'good morning,' I left them at full liberty to pump or sink, being satisfied that if they all took off their hats to bale, they would have sufficient employment without running after me. In about another half hour I landed safe, a short distance from Rye. And now, Charley, let us know what you did?"

"Well," said Charley, "here's your health, Captain. If any skipper knowed how to get out of a row you did; so when I woke up out of my morning's nap, I jumped up out of the forepeak, and there was I all alone, and the little Nancy with tiller lashed a lee, and the fore-sheet to windward.

"So I begin to look round me, and there I saw the cutter to leeward, and the six men rolling about the deck of the Nancy, moored head and starn, and swearing at me because I didn't cut them adrift. So Captain—I begins to think, and says I, now what's the reason I can't get away from that cutter?—the Nancy can run pretty well sometimes: and then says I again —I can come the Frenchman over them after all. So I let draw the fore-sheet, and aft I goes to the helm.

"'Cut me adrift!' roared out one.

"'*Non parlez Anglais,*' says I, and I shook my head as if I couldn't understand them. Presently a nice little breeze sprung up, a little to the southward of east,—I kept my luff, and the cutter, when she see what I was about, give sheet after me, and left her boat to get ashore as she could.

"It made me laugh, to see the revenue chaps, rolling and kicking about like Dutch doggers in the North Sea! The topsail was set, and the big jib, and all, and as the wind got up, we walked away from the cutter, though she was as big again as us; for the Nancy was only about forty tons. You never see a thing like it in your life; she seemed to fly, and the cutter was dropping astarn fast.

"Well, Captain, I knowed how to steer the Nancy, you know, and I watched her like I would a child. So I found I was getting too close in to Old Harry, and I was obliged to tack. So I put the helm down, and lashed it, jumped forrard and shifted over the jib, and let draw the foresail, and she never lost an inch by it."

"About ten o'clock, the breeze was just as much as I wanted; but an easterly wind always freshens as the sun gets up, you know, and I found she had just so much as she could stagger under. She shoved her gunwale under now and then, but that was nothing; all I cared about was the sticks; but thinks I, as long as the bowsprit holds on, I don't care much about the topmast. But by and by, a puff of wind took her, and brought the water up to the combings of the main hatchway, and crash goes the topmast, close down to the cap.

"I always said it was a bad stick, you know, Captain; I never did like them white spars, they never was good for anything yet, as I ever knowed off: I remember once losing three topmasts just like that one, in chace, when I belonged to the *La Forte*. But that's neither here nor there. So thinks I, I must shove her round again, and then I can clear away the wrack a littlematter;—for you see, the sail was dragging overboard to leeward, and stopping her way. So I shoved her round again, and brought the sail in board, and then let go the sheet, out knife and cut away, and I soon had the topsail on deck, as snug as could be:

jumping aft now and then to steady the helm.

"I carried on till about twelve o'clock, as near as I could guess by my inside; and as the cutter was a long way off, I jumped down into the cabin, and brought up a bottle of the right stuff; 'cause I felt a little matter dry." Here Charley 'stopped to freshen' hawse in reality.

"Well, my lads," continued he, wiping his mouth, "as I don't want to make a long story out of nothing, I took a pull now and then at the Nantz; but I minded my steerage for all that, and carried on while there was a chance left for me; but as the wind blew very strong at about two o'clock, the cutter out-carried me, and crawled up very fast, and when he got in gun shot, he fired at me.

"But it was all one, I wasn't the man to flinch at a dirty little four-pounder, and determined not to heave to. So I kept on, for full another hour, and by that time the cutter was close up on my lee quarter.

"'Heave to, you —— rascal!' hailed the

captain of the cutter; 'heave to, you scoundrel, or I'll shoot you through the head.

"'*Non parlez Anglais,*' says I. So he slapped off a musket, and the shot whistled close by my head.

"'*Oui monsieur,*' says I, and I shoved my helm hard a weather, run him right athwart hawse, and carried away his bowsprit. So half a dozen chaps jumped aboard, and I was 'bleedg'd to strike. They turned to and swore at me, as if I'd been a Turk, but I looked as knowing as could be, and says I, '*Non comprande.*'

"They cast off the heel and muzzle lashings of the poor devils as had been lying about the deck, and as wet as shags, and then they overhauled the craft, and a famous prize she was; only not half so good as if they had got men and all."

"Well, and what came of it?" asked Dick Slender, as soon as Charley had again moistened his throat.

"Why, they took her into Southampton, to be sure, and the next day, they hauled me up afore a justice of the peace, and wanted me to say I was an Englishman, and axed me a lot of questions. '*Non comprande*,' says I, 'cause you see, I had picked up a good lot of the lingo, whilst I was in the *fair trade*."

"But," asked Tim with surprise, "you didn't hail for a Frenchman—did you?"

"Yes," answered Charley, "that wasn't any harm, was it?"

"What!" replied Tim, looking marlin spikes through his single eye, which rolled about from side to side, as if it would unship itself. "Hail for a Frenchman! Why I would'nt do sich a thing as that—no, not to save me from being hanged."

"Nor I," said Fat Jack, and some others joined in. Poor Charley looked as if he had been committing murder.

"Hark'ee, shipmates!" exclaimed Dick Slender, "Charley's all right, so he did not fight for them. It's all right, my hearty," said he to Charley, " it's all fair in the *fair trade*."

"Why, as to the matter of being a Frenchman, shipmates, I am none, and I'd floor the fellow as called me such a thing; but I never thought it was wrong to hail for one when you could club-haul out of a five years' sarvice in a man-of-war. Not that I valued going into a man-of-war a ropeyarn; but all's one for that. So I badgers all hands for a long time, and thought I should have weathered them complete, but as they could'nt catch me on one tack, they tried me on another. So half-a-dozen fresh hands comes into the court-house, and one on 'em jumps up, and says he, ' That's George Jones, and he was borned in St. Giles's.'

" ' You're a d——d liar" says I, and afore the words was out of my mouth I knowed it was all up. I got into a terrible passion, 'cause the chaps shoved their tongues in their cheeks and laughed at me. I was sentenced to sarve five years in his Majesty's sarvice; and Miss Kitty, as I said, married a butcher. But I say, captain, let us hear something out of your log-book, for now, I 'sposes, we got nothing else to do but to tell long yarns and sing songs, and that like."

" Yes, sing us one of your foksel dittees, Charley," said Dick Slender coaxingly, " with a good swingeing chorus at the end of it." And Charley, without much pressing, favoured them with that excellent song of Dibdin's, called " I sailed from the Downs in the Nancy."

"But what's the reason, captain," asked Charley, "why you can't tell us what breeze brought you into this here port of ours? It seems good enough for the likes of us old hard-a-weathers.

"Why, Charley, it is a very long story, and you would all be asleep before I had got a tenth part through it; but I do not mind calling back old times, if you have a mind to listen to me. I have been playing at see-saw all my life time; sometimes up, and sometimes down in the world; for as soon as I succeeded in anything, some gale or other was sure to spring up, and leave me as bad off as before. I am not obliged to stop here; I could leave it to-morrow if I liked. But I am fond of my old friends here, and there is no one to care for me beside, that I know of. So some evening when you are in the humour, I will, to please you, give you a part of my history."

CHAPTER XIII.

*"Soft was his tone, and sober was his face,
Actions his words, and words his actions grace."*
                    Pope's *Homer's Iliad.*

The next evening being Sunday, was treated with too much respect by Tom Peters, to be made a time for story telling: age and experience had sobered him, and taught him the valuable lesson of religious belief; by which the actions of his latter years, whatever his early conduct might have been, were greatly governed.

To his friendship for Roberts, the reader is indebted for many facts which he did not choose to relate before all his wardmates; but as it would deprive the narrative of many of its alluring qualities, were it to be divided, I risk the blame which may be thrown upon me for incorrectness, when so great an advantage is in view.

Imagine therefore, gentle reader, a respectable old man, sitting before a cheerful fire, in a large arm-chair, and on each side of him, some seated on stools, and some on the long benches, a knot of listeners; and though you may picture to your mind's eye, some nodding, and others yawning and inattentive, yet if you know anything of the world, (I beg pardon for the *if,*) you must be aware that, such a fate often attends the speeches and narratives of many, whose claims on their hearers are considered very far superior to his.

The History of Tom Peters.

"I was born something less than sixty years back, in the little town of Lymington, where my father had lived many years. I was the youngest of seven boys, and as a natural consequence, was my poor indulgent mother's darling: I was therefore made a fool of until my eleventh year. No one dared to deny me anything, for my mother was always on my side, as I was never in her opinion in the wrong. But as I grew up, I found the misfortune of it.

"My poor mother died soon after I reached my eleventh year, and I soon found a great difference; for I had acquired in the few years I had lived a fondness for my own way, which no one seemed now inclined to yield to me.

"My father was an austere man, and I only liked him for his fondness to my poor mother. He often told her, in my hearing, that she was doing her best to make a fool of me; but her constant answer was, 'He is so young—he will be better as he gets older.'

"School was a restraint I did not approve of, so that at the age of twelve years, I was just learning to read. As my father now insisted on sending me with my brothers, I got on very well after the first, as I began to like learning; so in a short time, did a great deal.

"My brothers, with the exception of the next one to me, were like my father, proud,

and cruel; Jim was like my mother, kind
and affectionate. My father had in early life
been a sailor, but he had taken so great a dislike to everything nautical, that he would not
suffer any of us even to have playthings of that
kind, and threatened us with his severest dis-
pleasure if we ever went into a boat, except to
cross the ferry.

"As the 'rule of contrary,' was always a
greater favourite with me than the 'Rule of
Three,' I lost no time, after hearing my father one
day reprove me for my inclination that way, in
going down to the quay; where, finding a boat
belonging to a merchant vessel, made fast to a
ring bolt on the landing-place, I jumped into it,
and casting off the painter, shoved out into the
creek to have a little amusement.

"I liked the novelty very much, but found it
was much easier to get away than to get back
again, altho' I did my best endeavour to do so,
especially as the boy, in whose care the boat
was left, was calling upon me rather angrily to
return. The tide was running out sufficiently
strong to be carrying me away very fast, and if

a waterman, passing at the time, had not taken me in tow, and carried me back to the landing-place, I should very quickly have been stuck in the mud.

"As soon as I got out of the boat, the boy—you are the boy I mean, Charley—very unceremoniously gave me a thump at the side of the head; and as I was getting to be fourteen years of age, and a sturdy boy, I returned the compliment. You were some years older, and much stronger, but you remember we had a sharp, although short round, which ended in my rolling off the quay into the water, where I found myself striking out merrily,

"You soon repented of what you had done, for I remember it was you who pulled me out again; and although I was willing to renew the combat in the boat, you with great forbearance declined it.

"I was landed and walked home, when my father, not thinking my ducking, and the black eye I received, a sufficient punishment for my neglect of his injunctions, gave me a very severe beating, as soon as I had changed my clothes.

But what was still more galling to me, was that, my eldest brother, who was a clerk in a merchant's office, laughed at me, and taunted me with the pleasantness of my excursion. Jim took my part; but I thought myself able to take my own, and I ventured to reply to my elder brother's ridicule, by calling him a puppy, and a fool: this took place in the drawing-room, after my father had left.

"My brother, feeling the justice of the epithets I bestowed upon him, began beating me with his cane: my brothers looking on. My rage was at its greatest pitch, and so soon as I was released from the posture in which he had confined me, I flew to the first moveable that I could lift, which happened to be a small glass globe, containing gold and silver fish. This I lifted with both hands, and threw it right at him: the vessel struck his head, and falling on the floor, was shivered into a thousand pieces, giving the fish and the water full liberty to go where they pleased.

"My father entered just as I had performed this feat, and instead of inquiring into the circumstances, and thrashing my brother, he sentenced me to solitary confinement in my bedroom. It appeared to me that my father's conduct was unnatural and cruel; and I determined to free myself, in some way or other, from a repetition of it.

"I sat down when I was locked into my prison, and coolly concerted in my own mind a scheme of acting, in which I promised myself a great deal of revenge and happiness. So I waited until the clock struck eleven, and then knowing the household to be all asleep, I unlaced my bed sacking, and first trying the length out of the window, I made one end of it fast to the bed-post, and lowered myself, with a bravery I knew not I possessed, out of the window four stories high into the garden; receiving no other damage than knocking the skin off my knuckles.

"I had then to scale a wall, twelve feet high, which I accomplished; and having only forgotten a hat, I made all possible haste to the quay. Just as I reached that place, a vessel was in the act of hauling off, to go down the creek with the tide. I got on board unperceived, and finding one of the hatches off, I jumped down, and found myself amongst sacks of corn, stowed close up to the deck in the wings, and only sufficient room for me to move. The remaining hatch was soon afterwards put over, and I heard a bar placed across it, and a lock applied.

"I very soon found the place get unpleasantly close and warm; and although I would not allow myself to confess it, yet the thought struck me, that I had not made a good exchange. I crawled about as much as I could, and at last discovered a place, where there was a better chance of breathing.

"In a short time, I heard the men at work warping out; but falling asleep, I heard no more until awoke by the vessel's rolling about, and the thumping of a boat alongside.

"In a minute or two afterwards I heard some one unfastening the hatch bar, when, fearful of being discovered, I shoved myself into a snug berth between two sacks of corn, so that it was impossible for any one to see me. I had hardly completed my arrangements, when a man got down into the hold, declaring all the time the uselessness of looking; saying he was sure there was not room even for a mouse. Another person, who seemed to be still doubtful, and who I discovered to be my father, then jumped also into the hold; but he was soon convinced it was quite impossible I could be there; and after searching every other part of the vessel, I heard him get into the boat, in which he had left Lymington, and shove off. The vessel, as I afterwards learnt, was waiting for the tide to go through the Needles, and had anchored off 'Jack.'

"Soon afterwards I heard the men heaving up the anchor, and much to my joy found by the noise of the waves against the vessel's sides that we were going rapidly through the water.

"I went to sleep again after my father left, and was only awaked by a very unpleasant sensation in my inside, of which I could not conjecture the cause: this feeling increased with every pitch the vessel gave, and these motions were now numerous, and heavy. It occurred to me that a little fresh air would have the effect of reviving me, and that a little water would be very refreshing; but both, from being not easily obtainable, seemed doubly necessary and desirable.

"With all the strength of my lungs therefore, I roared out—'Let me out!' 'Let me out!' 'Let me out, or I shall die!' I might as well have been whistling jigs to a milestone all the while: for the boat, when hoisted in, had been placed right over the main hatchway, and a tarpaulin had been placed over them also, to keep the wet out.

"Like a poor cat, which some mischance has placed in a hole to starve, I continued to utter cries still fainter, and fainter, as assistance seemed further removed from me; when a heavy plunge of the vessel employed me in another way. Between whiles, as the vessel's comparative tranquillity left my inside alone, I renewed my cry, 'Let me out!' 'Let me out!'

"I continued passing my time in this manner for some hours, but the case appeared very hopeless, and I imagined myself doomed to undergo suffocation. While, however, a gasp remained to me, nature prompted my continuance of calling—' Let me out!' ' Let me out!' ' I shall die!' and then I added a scream. At last finding a whistle in my pocket, I played a tune upon it: and by the latter means I was fortunate enough to be brought to light.

" I soon heard the men asking one of another where the noise came from; and upon this I repeated my whistling, and screaming; and to my very great satisfaction, I soon found they were lifting the boat, and unfastening the hatches.

" ' Holloa! where did you spring from,' said one of the men, as he caught hold of me, and pulled me up out of the hold, with a face and jacket as white as a miller,—half dead with fright and sea-sickness.

" ' Why! it's young Master ——!' said the master of the vessel—' why, how did you find your way there?'

" ' Give me something to drink!' I exclaimed pettishly, when Charley there, assisted me to the parish pot, belonging to the scuttle butt. I looked at my cup bearer with much surprise, but no resentment; the sea-sickness had quite tamed me, and made me careless of everything. The master of the vessel treated me with every attention; he took me below to his cabin, put me in his own bed, and I received every mark of respect from him and the crew.

"I learnt that the vessel was bound to Carnarvon, for a cargo of slates, of which I was very glad; and as the sea-sickness soon left me, by the time we had rounded the Lands-end, I had been very close to her truck, and before we reached Carnarvon, could lend a hand to reef the mainsail.

"I felt great uneasiness at the thought that I should be carried back again to Lymington; as I considered my father would not like me any better for the voyage I had undertaken. The master, however, wrote and informed him of my safety, desiring to know what was to be done with me; and in the meantime, as there was no chance of my escaping from Carnarvon, I was suffered to go on shore and walk about the town.

"I was particularly fond of the old castle, and was continually finding out some new passage, or some dungeon darker than the rest.

I peopled some of them in my young imagination, and gave to each of them a ghost. I would crawl through places which must have been used as drains, and was never more delighted than when it terminated in some deep, and black hole, always carefully avoiding pitching into it head over heels.

"Charley and I were very soon excellent friends, although we generally had a fight once in the twenty-four hours; and one day I obtained the master's leave for him to go on shore with me for a walk. As the castle and its subterranean passages, had so many beauties for me, I supposed Charley would like them as well; and I proposed shewing him into a dungeon, where the music of the toads, together with the clanking of chains, produced a fine concert.

"Making sure, as I thought, of my road, I entered one of the passages just under the tower still standing, called, I think, the 'Eagle Tower,' and after walking a little way, it gradually narrowed until we got on our hands and knees. We crawled on, and groped our way in darkness, Charley being close behind me, praying me not to go any farther."

"I was never so frightened in all my life," said Charley.

"So it seemed," continued Peters; "but as I expected soon to get to the dungeon, I did not heed what he said, but kept creeping along, the aperture gradually narrowing.

"'Come back for God's sake, young master,' exclaimed Charley; 'I hears the toads, and the chains now,—do, pray, let us go back.'

"Just at that moment, a whole gang of rats, as if running a race, passed us at full speed, and Charley screamed aloud with terror. His screams were answered by a thousand echoes, and the noise was really terrible. Charley could not stand it, and he swooned away.

"I was never so before," said Charley.

"I was perhaps as much frightened, though I did not swoon; yet wishing to retreat, I found it was impracticable, as my way was blocked up by Charley's inanimate body.

"At this trying moment I had recourse to an entire new method to compass Charley's recovery, and it proved much more efficacious than salts, hartshorn, burnt paper, or feathers, or any other remedy ever heard of. I commenced kicking him with all my force, some of which kicks touched his head, and some his shoulders; and one drew blood from his nose.

"Nothing could be more surprising than the effect of this novel manner of treatment on poor Charley. After a very few applications, he commenced swearing at me, and after a few more, he was able to make a retrograde movement; so that we soon returned to broad daylight.

"My patient was very ungrateful, although I acknowledge he did but pay his debt, and in my own coin; for as soon as we were at liberty, he attacked me furiously, for the kicking I had given him, and returned me some of the blows with interest at cent. per cent. We had a set-to of course, which lasted near half an hour, resting every now and then, and anon renewing the battle: at the end of which time, we were again the best of friends. Charley has never forgotten that adventure, and has often talked it over with me.

" The master of the vessel received an answer from my father by return of post, desiring him to take care of me, and bring me back again when he returned, provided he could not find an earlier conveyance; and while the vessel was reloading, I had ample opportunities of seeing everything to be seen at Carnarvon, and of partaking of the hospitality of some of the families of that most hospitable part of the world.

" I was much struck with their language; and it puzzled me extremely to hear them talking sometimes Welsh, sometimes English: it seemed scarcely possible for the same tongue to pronounce both the languages.

" Our cargo being at length completed, I left that place with much regret. We sailed, and anchored again in Studwell roads, from which, with a number of other coasting vessels, we departed under convoy of a gun-brig.

" I have all my lifetime been Fortune's plaything: most are so, who, as I did, have thrown themselves completely in her power. Having rounded the Lizard with a fair wind, we were working up Channel; when a fine dashing frigate, with her white sails, and bright well-painted sides, brought the convoy to. 'Oh!' I exclaimed, 'what a beautiful ship! how I should like to sail in such a vessel!'

"At this time I had never been near to any vessel of war, except the old gun-brig that convoyed us; between which, and the merchant ships, there was not a great deal of difference. I jumped about the deck, and capered with delight, having never seen anything to please me half so much.

"Not so the men,—who would as soon have seen the devil; and the mate and two men, who were liable to be pressed, ran below, leaving only Charley, the captain, and myself on deck. One of them hid himself in the mainhold among the slates, while the mate got into the sail-locker abaft, and another stowed himself away under the captain's bed."

CHAPTER XIV.

"So adieu! to the white cliffs of Britain,
　Our girls and our dear native shore,
For if some hard rock we should split on,
　We shall never see them any more."—*Sea Song*.

"A BOAT from the frigate then came alongside, having boarded two or three other vessels, and a dashing young fellow, with a cocked-hat and sword, jumped on board, and ordered the master to send his men aft to be mustered. 'Aye, aye, sir, it's all very well for you to order me to send my men aft,' said the master, 'but I should like to know where I'm to find 'em. I can tell you, if you want them to come aft, you must fetch 'em.'

"A great many words ensued; but as the master stated his inability to bring his men up, half a dozen of the cutter's crew were ordered out of the boat, and a general search took place; but whether the searchers did not like their job, or whether the hiding places were difficult to detect, they only succeeded in finding one, poor John Simmons, after a half an hour's overhaul. John pleaded a wife and family at Lymington; but it was all one; he was ordered to get his traps up, and put them in the boat.

"By this time the frigate appearing impatient of the delay, hoisted the boat's recal, and she was just about to shove off in obedience to the signal, when I, who had been employing myself, gaping with astonishment and pleasure at the boat alongside, and its clean fine-looking crew, saw that I should lose my chance of joining her if I did not speak. So, just as the lieutenant was getting into the boat, I said to him, 'Will you have me?'

"'Yes, to be sure,' replied the officer, 'jump in;' and I took him at his word, saying to the master as the boats hoved off, 'Good bye, old chap—tell my old Dad, I'm gone for a cruize.'

"The master expostulated with the officer, telling him I was the owner's son; but the boat's signal of recal was enforced by a gun, and the voice of the master of the Ann was soon lost in the distance.

"As we neared this 'beautiful specimen of art,' (as the newspaper people say,) with her guns projecting in fearful array from her checkered sides—the white tompions looking like cannon-balls; my boyish feelings of love of novelty were gratified. I little thought of consequences then, and I believe I have not gained much knowledge in that line since.

"My conversation with the officer in the boat consisted of very few words. He asked me how long I had been at sea, and whether I could go aloft to furl a royal. In answer to the first I said 'a month,' and to the second, 'I should *think* so !'

"As may be supposed, my superfine jacket and trowsers, from the nature of my employment, had assumed a very sailor-like appearance, they being covered with tar and grease, and such like, from clue to earing. I had also borrowed one of Charley's shirts, and a tarpaulin hat substituted the one I had left at home. I was rather tall for my age, and what spoke more in my favour was, that I cared for nothing.

"As soon as the boat touched the ship's side, I jumped up, and was two or three steps up the ship's side, when I was unceremoniously pulled back into the boat, by the coxswain, who asked me, 'where I learnt my manners?' and abused me for attempting to get out before the officer.

"I however followed him close at his heels, and notwithstanding the pulls and twitches I received from one and the other, walked aft with him, as he went to report himself to a very gentlemanly-looking man, rather tall and thin, but who wore a short jacket.

"The lieutenant raised his hat, and said, 'Come on board, sir.'

"'So it seems, sir. And what have you been doing,' replied the captain, angrily.

"'I have got two men, and a boy, sir,' answered the lieutenant; but as the conversation did not interest me nearly so much as the hoisting up the quarter-boat, which had been dropped astern and hooked on, as soon as we had got out of her, I jumped up on one of the guns to look over the hammock netting, thinking I should witness the process to greater advantage.

"I was enjoying the scene very much: the boat was rising up beautifully, and the boatswain's mate had just piped belay, when I was warned by a very unpleasant feeling on my *western side*,* (as the pure Americans call it,) that the master-at-arms in the H—— carried a thing called—a cane.

"I had not learnt to be more patient than when I threw the globe of fish at my brother's head, nor had I learnt the folly of resistance on board a man-of-war. I therefore looked hastily round in the first place, to ascertain the cause of the stroke, secondly, to rub the part affected, and thirdly, to seek the readiest means of revenge.

"As there was no handspike near enough, I thought my head would serve my purpose, and as the master-at-arms had retreated a short

---

* See Captain Marryatt's Naval Officer.

distance, I made a spring off the gun, and directing my head at his stomach—he was rather corpulent—they came in contact with such force as to make him stagger back a few steps, and his heel catching a bight of a rope, he measured his length on the deck.

"Captain ——— could laugh sometimes, and especially when he was pleased. The ludicrous appearance of the master-at-arms, who like a cockroach on his back, was trying to get his right side up again, made him forget the breach of discipline I had been guilty of, and from a very ill state of temper, give way to a violent fit of laughter, in which he was joined by the lookers-on.

"I stood up like a Trojan, believing I had achieved a very glorious action; but at the same time, I could not avoid rubbing the part affected, although the smart was greatly lessened by the revenge I had obtained for it.

"As soon as the laughter of Captain ——— had subsided, he asked the lieutenant where he had picked me up, and then he beckoned me towards him.

"'What's your name, youngster?' asked he: so I told him.

"'Who do you belong to?' said he.

"'Any body—you if you like,' replied I.

"'This is a bright article,' added he, turning to the first lieutenant. 'Come here, sir,' for I was keeping a sort of respectful distance from him. 'Do you know where you are, sir?'

"'No, that indeed I don't, s-i-r,' hesitating whether a man with a short jacket on deserved so much respect.

"'Then you will soon find out,' he answered. 'Who was your father—do you know?'

"'Mr. ——— of Lymington,' said I.

"'Indeed, I knew him very well some years back; and did you run away from him?'

"'Yes, sir."

"'And what for?'

"'Because I could not do as I liked,' said I.

"'Then,' said the Captain, 'do you expect to do as you like here?'

At this I said nothing. He then asked me what I wanted to be—what clothes I had belonging to me—and a number of other questions. An inventory of my clothes was not necessary, and as to rating, I said I wanted to be a sailor.

"During this dialogue, I never altered my position, nor moved my hat. I had then no idea as to what a Captain of a man-of-war was. I did not know that he was one of the most absolute of monarchs; and as I found these things out, it did not inspire me with any great increase of love, although I was induced to pay proper deference to his authority.

"A gentleman with a pale face, and a large book, which he placed upon the capstan, then asked me a number of questions concerning my name, age, parentage, place of nativity, &c. &c. my answers to which he wrote down in the book. The Captain told him to give me a rating as a midshipman, and overruled all objections about my outfit, by ordering that the chest of a midshipman, left behind at Plymouth, should be transferred to me; and with a kindness which he could show when he pleased, he placed me under the special care of the caterer Mr. Hopkins.

"Mr. Hopkins was an excellent creature, and a good officer. He was fond of 'moistening his clay,' but his good nature, and general attention to his duty, made up all other deficiencies. Grown bald in the service, which he had entered nearly twenty years before, he bore the unfortunate title of 'an old master's mate.' To be an *old master's mate*, implied drunkenness, or some other vice; since, had the case been otherwise, it was argued he would have been promoted long before.

"Mr. Hopkins's face was scarred with the small pox; he had sandy whiskers, and light hair; and when the captain called him up from below, he was attired in a garb by no means becoming a gentleman. He had come out of the spirit-room, and his jacket was whitened at the back and elbows, and his large pig-tail had received a like embellishment.

"This the Captain looked over, knowing Mr. Hopkins to be mate of the lower deck. I was transferred to his care, and with him marched below.

"Everything was a matter of surprise to me.

The main deck with its never ending tier of guns, and the taught shining black ridge-rope passed along fore and aft,—the racks of muskets,—the fire buckets and match tubs,—every thing which my eye rested upon was a subject of wonder to me.

"As I reached the lower deck, and was ushered into the midshipman's berth on the larboard side, where a few of the gentlemen were assembled, I looked round as well as the darkness would permit me, and perceived something like a white table-cloth upon the table, laid out with plates and knives and forks, and that there was some expectation entertained of getting a dinner.

"There were several young men walking about in the steerage, who each hailed me with a significant look, and occasionally I heard myself compared to a 'young bear, whose sorrows were all to come.'

"I had been used to dirty trenchers, &c. on board the Ann; but I considered those I had to use for dinner were much dirtier. However, as I was never very particular, I thought I could make them do; and at the request of my protector the caterer, I seated myself, and began playing with my knife and fork.

"In a few minutes the bell struck eight, and as the welcome music of the boatswain and his mates, which greatly excited my admiration, dismissed the men to their dinners, they came rushing down, and in a minute the lower deck presented a busy scene indeed.

"The midshipman's berth was soon filled, and the table covered with a dish of *salt hog*, peas-soup, and *dogsbody*,* a dish of potatoes in their skins, and a basket of biscuit. The drinking-vessels were of dingy glass, a black-jack held water, and lime-juice bottles contained the rum.

"They were all very kind to me, when they knew I had some pretensions to the gentleman;

---

* As every one may not know exactly what is meant by this *elegant* term, it is necessary to remark, that it is a preparation of refractory, or hard peas, which are taken out of the coppers, and bruised between two pieces of wood, fastened together by a thong of leather, called *dog's-body squeezers*, similar to the machine used for squeezing elder berries.

they asked me a number of questions; but the only answer I could obtain, when I asked them if it was not a very pleasant employment, was one which I have often thought of since,—' They who go to sea for pleasure, ought to go to h—ll for pastime.'

"The frigate I had by such an odd chance been thrown into, was just fitted out, and was bound to the West Indies. Her captain was a perfect gentleman in his manner, yet among the men he bore the worst of characters; but 'the devil,' they say, ' is not so black as he is painted,' and I can say of that unfortunate man that he had *some* good qualities. They were, however, completely overbalanced by his total want of temper, and especially after dinner.

"He would sometimes come up out of his cabin, and stand clear! for the first one near him would be the object of his abuse.

"He would turn the hands up, rig the gratings on both sides, and flog away both sides together. But the worst of all was his practice of starting. I have known a poor fellow have his body covered with the bruises inflicted by a broomstick, or the end of the fore-brace, merely because he might have checked an inch too much or too little of a rope he had been ordered to attend to.

"He was for a time tolerably kind to me, and as I became more acquainted with my situation and my duty, I got on very well; for as soon as I knew the impropriety of not paying respect to my superiors in rank, I altered my conduct, and rose considerably in their estimation.

CHAPTER XV.

"I will instruct my sorrow to be proud,
For grief is proud, and makes his owner stout."
SHAKSPEARE.

"Let me die where I am! and as the fuel
Of life shrunk in his heart, and thick and sooty
The drops fell from his death-wound, and drew ill
His breath,—he from his swelling throat untied
A kerchief, crying, 'Give Sal that!'—and died."
BYRON.

"AMONG my messmates was one of a very overbearing disposition, who was continually taunting me with the circumstances attending my being forced upon them, as he called it; and as I was rather impatient, I retorted in good set terms; repeating what I had heard respecting his birth—whether it was true or false, I know not—and telling him I had much more right to the situation of a *gentleman* than himself. Words ensued, he struck me, and I returned the blow. There was an uproar directly; but my messmates in the end decided that I was entitled to satisfaction if I wanted it. Accordingly, the table was unshipped and the berth cleared, to make room for us to fight it out.

"My antagonist was near seventeen, but no taller than myself, only much stouter. We stripped off our jackets, and set to work in good earnest. My lessons with Charley had been of much service to me, and as the majority sided with me, I was going on very well, and had blackened one of my opponent's eyes. Determined not to be beaten, he made a desperate attempt to grapple with me, and give me a fall. In this I was his match, and we both came down, but he was underneath, and the corner of a liquor case being in the way, the contact cut open his head, and nearly fractured his skull.

"There he lay stunned. The doctor's mate being at hand, immediately bled him, restored him again, and all would have been well, as I give the young man the credit of not wishin me any serious injury, had it not been for my friend the master-at-arms, who coming to put out the lights, heard what was going on, and as I was a principal performer, he, with a great deal of pleasure, reported the affair to the first lieutenant.

"It so happened that, when the circumstance was reported to the captain, he was in one of his angry moods, and ordered me to be *flogged!* To this source I may trace the cause of the recklessness which marked many of my after actions. My naturally violent temper might have been curbed by kindness, but was not to be subdued by disgrace!

"At this moment, I fancy I hear the order to 'tie me up to the gun!' But the devilish feeling which for years afterwards, and even to this hour, caused by that degradation, has ever, and will ever follow me. The name of *gentleman* has been gall to me ever since. I am no gentleman! I am——"

"You're a man though," said Charley, rising up, and taking Tom's hand, (who had worked his feelings up to a painful pitch by the recurrence of this portion of his reminiscences,) " and that's more than many of them as hails for *gen'lmen* can say."

" I am a fool, said Tom," continuing his story, " but I could have borne anything but disgrace; and if the author of it had not met with a more horrible fate, I would have shot him, and mine alone should have been the crime, and punishment.

" I went below, stripped myself of every article of clothing which belonged to the chest I had been intrusted with, and rigged myself in my old tarry clothes, and hat. These at least, thought I, are left me, and never will I in this ship appear again as an officer. I never went into the midshipman's berth afterwards, but, finding a vacancy in John Simmons' mess forward, I was allowed to join it.

The captain ordered me to be disrated, and I was stationed along with Simmons in the foretop. I soon began to know my duty, and to like my situation. I felt at home with the blunt honest fellows, who would have done anything to serve me. They were all of a mind; no quarrelling among them; they stuck together, and the more so as they were persecuted.

"It takes a great deal to make a sailor mutiny: it is not done by merited punishment. A sailor knows as well as his officers do, when he deserves flogging; but if he knows he does not deserve it, every lash cuts deeper than the flesh, and leaves a scar which it takes a long time to wear out, if it is ever effaced. Men in that ship were expected to do what was impossible: a whole watch of fore-topmen would sometimes be flogged for being a few seconds after the main-topmen, and the last man on the topsail yard was sure of it.

"John Simmons was second captain of the top, and as smart a sailor as ever hauled out a reef-earing. One evening, some time after my being disrated, I was aft at the lee helm, as there was a fresh breeze of wind. The captain came upon deck, and I could see by his detested face, that the devil was in him: his nostrils were compressed, and his upper lip curled up in a scroll. He took two or three short and hurried turns—looked aloft, and swore at the officer of the watch, for having slacked off the lee fore-topsail brace,—called the quarter-master an old lubber, and gave certain symptoms of the return of his madness.

"He then roared out, 'Turn the hands up, reef topsails, and I'll flog the last half-dozen on the lower deck.' The men came rushing up from below as though the devil himself had been driving them.

"'Now,' said he, taking out his watch, 'I allow you one minute, and I'll flog every man of you if you are not in time,—'way aloft, lower away the topsails.' The men flew up the rigging like lightning, and, the command, 'trice up, lay out, take in two reefs'—was hardly given, when it seemed the sail was reefed, the men off the yard, and the sail at the mast-head again. It was done within the time allotted, but on looking up, a point was discovered untied, in both fore and main-topsails.

"The captain very *humanely* gave them another trial, and the reefs were shaken out and the sail reefed, as quickly, and as well as before; but, poor John, who was at the lee yard-arm, in his anxiety to avoid being the last man on the yard, made a spring at the lee rigging, he missed his hold, and fell upon the deck!—poor fellow! every bone in his skin was broken!

"'What —— lubber is that?' demanded the captain, of the forecastle officer.

"'The second captain of the fore-top, sir,'—replied the lieutenant.

"'Pitch him overboard and be —— then,' returned the captain.

"This horrid mandate was not obeyed; the doctor was aft, and ran forward to see what could be done; but his promptitude was useless: poor John was dying.

"When he fell, I was close by him, and ran to him, and raising his head gently from the deck, supported it on my arm. The doctor wished him to be removed to the sick-bay, but he said faintly, 'Don't touch me—good bye, shipmates—God bless you all'—and as the glaze was coming over his eyes, he recognised me, and his last whisper was—'poor Jane—give—give——,' his head fell back powerless on my arm, and he yielded up his last breath.

"'Shipmates,' murmured a hollow sepulchral voice close at hand, '*remember!*'

CHAPTER XVI.

"I'll read you matter deep and dangerous;
As full of peril and adventurous spirit
As to o'erwalk a current roaring loud,
On the unsteadfast footing of a spear."
SHAKSPEARE.

"HAD you witnessed the countenances of the men on the lower deck at supper that night, you would never have forgotten it: I never have; and although perfectly ignorant of what was in contemplation, I saw they were at the highest pitch of desperation.

"That night, poor John Simmons was sewed up in his hammock: the officer of the watch read the funeral service over him, by the light of a lanthorn, and as the awful words, 'We therefore commit his body to the deep,' pealed upon my ears, and the sullen roar of the waves as they received the corpse, which followed, the same voice before mentioned, in a still more awful manner, called out ' *Remember!*'

"The officer of the watch looked round him before he recommenced reading the latter part of the service, but all the men near him appeared to be as ignorant, as to whom the sound came from, as himself. A solemn ' Amen,' was pronounced, echoed by the same voice, which concluded this affecting and melancholy ceremony.

" I think it was the next day, (a man of war brig, the D——, was in company,) I observed several of the men going from one mess to the other, whispering something. One in particular, a man who had been a boatswain's mate, but disrated and flogged, because the captain thought he was not laying on the lash as he ought to have done, was very active. It was his voice I am almost certain that I had heard repeat the word—' remember;' but everything was so conducted that I knew nothing of what was brewing.

"It was the night for scrubbing and washing clothes, always done in the middle watch. I was between two of the guns abaft on the main deck, scrubbing a pair of duck trowsers. I thought there was an unusual noise with the wash-deck buckets, and looking up, I saw several of the men apparently larking, throwing the buckets at one another.

"The captain sent out of his cabin word for the men to make less noise, but they took no notice of what was said; on the contrary, they made more noise than before, taking the shot out of the racks, and throwing them about the deck.

"At last the first lieutenant came up, to enquire into the cause of the disturbance, when one of the men insulted him. He returned to his cabin and brought up a sword, with which he went forward amongst the men, and endeavoured to restore order. He was knocked down, run through the body with his own sword, and thrown out of a port.

"Seeing this horrid murder, I left my trowsers unfinished, ran on deck, and aloft to the main-top. From this place I heard the shouts of the infuriated mutineers, and the groans of the dying; and every now and then, the splash of some mangled victim, committed to the waves. The men had broken open the gunner's store-room, and possessed themselves of arms and ammunition.

"The captain, hearing the uproar increase, opened the cabin door, and came out. He was no sooner seen, than one of the men gave him a blow with a handspike, and he retreated to his cabin. Four or five of the men rushed in after him, armed with cutlasses, boarding pikes, and muskets with fixed bayonets. The captain endeavoured to defend himself with a short sword, and for a time kept them at bay. So much did they dread him, that they shrunk back, and were afraid to strike; when one of them—John Morris—called out, 'What do you fear, men? spike the ——,' and gave them an example by running him through with a bayonet. They all followed his example, each one seeming anxious to satiate his bloody vengeance. He was covered with a hundred wounds, and after cutting and hacking the body, and treating it with every possible indignity, they threw him out of the cabin windows.

"My late antagonist—if it was done on my account, I am very sorry—was another of their victims, and only two or three of the officers were exempted from the carnage; among them was a midshipman, and at the time sick in his cot: his life was saved by one of the mutineers, who was his countryman.

"I was soon joined by two or three others of the peaceably disposed, who, like me, were horror struck at the bloodshed going on below; and we did not quit our station until after the day broke.

"The main deck was covered with blood: it was the blood of our officers, many of whom were as good men as ever lived. I have often, since that time, stood upon a bloody deck, and thought light of it, for it was blood shed in our country's cause, and in fair fight. As to the captain, if he had possessed a thousand lives, he deserved to have lost them; but bloodthirsty cruelty alone, called for the murder of the rest.

"A boatswain's mate now took the command, and called a council of war. Some were for cruizing for prizes as a pirate; some wished to leave the West Indies, and take the ship into a French port; but the greatest number voted to run her into the first port they came to on the Spanish Main, and give her up to the Spaniards. The latter plan was carried into effect, and the next day found us at anchor under the guns of a heavy battery.

"Completely disgusted with the brutal riots of the men, now that all restraint was removed from them, I walked about the decks, alone, and wretched. The scene I had witnessed made me sick, as it recurred to me, and I earnestly longed for the time to come when I should be able to quit the polluted ship.

"As soon, therefore, as I had an opportunity, —which did not happen until the day after we arrived,—I went on shore; but, without money or friends, I knew not what to do with myself. I lingered about the quay in hopes of finding some employment, and observing one day a xebeque getting underway, I swam off to her, and got alongside just as she was getting fresh way on her. I scrambled up the side, and the Spanish captain received me kindly, ordering me to be fed, and supplied with dry clothes.

"I did not know a word of Spanish, but as there were two of the mutineers my shipmates on board, one of whom knew the language, the difficulty was removed. I confess I wished myself on shore again, as I did not at all like the faces of the gang around me, and least of all those of the Englishmen; it was, however, too late to think of that, and I determined to make the best of it I could. I felt happy that I was at least out of the company of the many lawless fellows who were doubly riotous from the restraint they had been accustomed to. But I had much to learn.

"The vessel was of about eighty tons, and armed with a long 18-pounder in midships, on a pivot, and four broadside guns, long sixes, or 4-pounders; with a crew composed of men of all nations, in all about sixty. The captain and officers were Spanish.

"Having neither bed nor bedding, I was obliged to sleep on the deck, with no protection against the heavy dews and night-air. But I was too hardy to mind that. The food, too, disgusted me very much at first; but to that I also soon became accustomed. The garlic, so valuable and essential to Spanish taste, was plentifully mixed with everything we had to eat, and I found jerked beef to be much inferior to 'king's own.'

"At noon one day, I stood by the *piloto* as he was taking the sun, and he had no sooner allowed me to read the altitude, than I told him the latitude so quickly that he was astonished. He was much pleased, and after that he took a great deal of notice of me, and always lent me his cloak at night, which was of great service to me, as the nights were often very cold.

"The pilot was rather an old man, and particularly fond of smoking; and so careful was he not to waste any portion of his segar, that when it was consumed to a very small piece, he would chew the rest. As his books were at my service, I, by the help of his instruction, acquired in a little time a very good knowledge of navigation.

"The doctor was a great friend of mine. He was a young man, with raven black hair, of very amiable and gentlemanly manners, and I could in a short time understand and speak sufficient of Spanish to enable me to converse with him.

"The captain's good will I gained, by my agility in getting out to the end of the long latteen yard, in a fresh breeze of wind, and when the vessel was knocking about a great deal. But an incident occurred, after we had been about a fortnight out, which rendered me very uncomfortable. One calm morning, a strange sail was discovered a long way off, and the sweeps were got out to enable us to close her. Our vessel rowed twelve sweeps of a side, and went at the rate of from three to four knots. The stranger was soon made out to be a merchant-schooner, and after pulling about four hours, we were pretty close up with the chace, when a light breeze of wind sprung up.

"It was one of those lovely mornings such as are only to be witnessed in that climate; for though the sun was shedding his brightest rays upon us, they were mild to us, being tempered by the atmosphere and cooling breeze. I cannot help talking a little on this subject when I think of the West Indies. Many years afterwards, I stood at the side of a dying shipmate, as he lay in his cot on the deck; he turned and looked out of the port at the green hills, and said to me in a sort of whisper, ' Oh ! Sir, what a beautiful world is this ! See how fresh all nature looks ! indeed, it is hard to leave it for the depths of the ocean !'

" But not to depart from my story, I must tell you that we rapidly neared the schooner, which was becalmed. Our captain ran right alongside, and ordered the men to board. No resistance was offered, the schooner being a Spanish merchant vessel, said to be from Carthagena, bound to Trinidad.

" I boarded her as well as the rest, out of curiosity, and our captain ordered the men to make a general search. She appeared to be laden with grain and jerked beef only; but he seemed to suspect her to have gold also.

" The captains had a great many angry

words, during which a pistol was more than once presented at the head of the defenceless captain of the schooner; but in the end our captain sent some men down to overhaul the cabin.

"The men succeeded in opening a small hatchway in the cabin floor, and beneath it they found gold and silver of great value, in bars, dollars, and doubloons. This discovery sealed the fate of the captain and crew of the schooner. Some were tied back to back, and thrown overboard, and it was truly horrible to behold their struggles, each endeavouring to be uppermost, and rolling over and over in their fruitless attempts, while their inhuman murderers laughed at their sufferings. Others were made to walk to the end of a plank projecting a long way from the vessel's side, when its inner end was lifted up, and the miserable wretch precipitated into the ocean.

"Thus, they all, to the number of about twenty, perished, and the schooner, a beautiful vessel, which, had there been any wind, we should never have caught, was then ransacked of everything valuable, scuttled before we quitted her, and down she went.

"I had now sufficient evidence of the character of the people about me, among the worst of which were the Englishmen. It was Morris who suggested the inhuman plan of tying the men back to back, and who was the most active in scuttling the vessel. But he had something else in view.

"Morris said to me one night,—it was after we had been out more than two months— 'Youngster,' said he, 'I think I could put you in the way of making your fortune if you knew navigation.'

"I replied that I did know quite enough for ordinary purposes. But as our conversation was broken in upon by the approach of some one, it was stopped. A short time after this, I was on the look-out forward, and Morris and the other man, whose name was Charles Mills, were sitting on the heel of the bowsprit, engaged in earnest talk.

"One of them said, 'He can navigate; he told me so.' I became interested. 'I have got the boatswain over,' said the other, 'and I think the pilot is inclined towards us.'

"'D——n him,' returned the first speaker, who I discovered to be Morris, 'that is the first —— I'd shoot.'

"'Well, well,' responded Mills, 'as you like, only let me know in time, that's all.'

"I could not catch any more, but I had heard enough to satisfy me that mischief was afloat, and I only wished I had it in my power to inform the captain; which, however, would have been certain death to me, as Morris was a favourite. Yet, to say truth, the horrid scenes of butchery I was daily witnessing, made me careless of what happened, and I looked upon that to be the most desirable which would soonest free me from my present brutal associates.

END OF VOL. I.

LONDON:
PRINTED BY STEWART AND MURRAY,
OLD BAILEY.